AF323643

WORLD IN TRANSITION

SINGAPORE'S FUTURE

IPS-NATHAN LECTURES

WORLD IN TRANSITION

SINGAPORE'S FUTURE

CHAN HENG CHEE

Published by

World Scientific Publishing Co. Pte. Ltd.

5 Toh Tuck Link, Singapore 596224

USA office: 27 Warren Street, Suite 401-402, Hackensack, NJ 07601

UK office: 57 Shelton Street, Covent Garden, London WC2H 9HE

National Library Board, Singapore Cataloguing in Publication Data
Names: Chan, Heng Chee.
Title: World in transition : Singapore's future / Chan Heng Chee.
Other titles: IPS-Nathan Lectures.
Description: Singapore : World Scientific Publishing Co Pte Ltd, [2021] |
   Includes bibliographic references and index.
Identifiers: OCN 1229081217 | ISBN 978-981-12-3445-3 (paperback) |
   ISBN 978-981-12-3421-7 (hardcover)
Subjects: LCSH: Singapore--Politics and government. | Singapore--Foreign relations. |
   United States--Foreign relations--China. | China--Foreign relations--United States.
Classification: DDC 320.95957--dc23

British Library Cataloguing-in-Publication Data
A catalogue record for this book is available from the British Library.

For any available supplementary material, please visit
https://www.worldscientific.com/worldscibooks/10.1142/12206#t=suppl

Desk Editor: Ong Shi Min Nicole

THE S R NATHAN FELLOWSHIP FOR THE STUDY OF SINGAPORE

AND THE IPS-NATHAN LECTURE SERIES

The S R Nathan Fellowship for the Study of Singapore was established by the Institute of Policy Studies (IPS) in 2013 to support research on public policy and governance issues. With the generous contributions of individual and corporate donors, and a matching government grant, IPS raised around S$5.9 million to endow the Fellowship.

Each S R Nathan Fellow, appointed under the Fellowship, delivers a series of IPS-Nathan Lectures during his or her term. These public lectures aim to promote public understanding and discourse on issues of critical national interest.

The Fellowship is named after Singapore's sixth and longest-serving President, the late S R Nathan, in recognition of his lifetime of service to Singapore.

Other books in the IPS-Nathan Lecture series:

The Idea of Singapore: Smallness Unconstrained
by Tan Tai Yong

The Ocean in a Drop — Singapore: The Next Fifty Years
by Ho Kwon Ping

Dealing with an Ambiguous World
by Bilahari Kausikan

The Challenges of Governance in a Complex World
by Peter Ho

Can Singapore Fall? Making the Future for Singapore
by Lim Siong Guan

Seeking a Better Urban Future
by Cheong Koon Hean

CONTENTS

FOREWORD

In 2019 when I was approached by IPS Director Janadas Devan to be the 7th S R Nathan Fellow, he asked if I could speak on the unravelling of institutions occurring in the world. He left that thought to my interpretation and imagination. As it happened, I had been mulling over the state of the world for some time. Having joined the Singapore University of Technology and Design, I have been moving in the space of disruption — whether it is in the economy, society or politics and geopolitics — with a keen sense of what technology and in particular artificial intelligence (AI) can do to transform and upend our lives, the way we work and go about our business, and how we can harness this new asset to bring the world to a better place. Technology can also precipitate the reshuffle of the order of hierarchy of nations although it would not be the only trigger. Other drivers of change have consequences too. I got used to factoring the idea of change and shock in my analyses, not just vaguely, intellectually, but applying its meaning in scenarios. So, I welcomed the opportunity to share my thoughts with Singaporeans.

The fact that we may be at an inflexion point in history, where significant changes could be underway, came home to me dramatically about a decade ago. I could not help recalling what a contrasting picture it was for me to think of the United States in 1996 when I arrived in the United States as Singapore's Ambassador to Washington, and in 2012 when I left my post. In 1996, American power was at its height. The United States was the world's hegemon. The Soviet Union had collapsed, and the United States and the West had won the Cold War. Around 1999, on the eve of the millennium, an exercise was conducted by the Center for Naval Analysis for Pentagon on certainties in the 21st century. I was one of the few foreign diplomats present, possibly because I was known to be someone from the academic and think tank world. As the couple of hundred participants typed on our computers, the master screen overhead captured our thoughts fast and furious. Statement after statement asserted confidently, "America will remain the world's hegemon", "The United States will be the only superpower in the world", etc. There were many variations of this idea. "Science will be king". There were statements about the growing dominance of technology. For many minutes into the exercise, there was not a line about China. So I entered, "In the 21st century China will emerge as a great power". I had debated whether I should type "superpower" or "great power", but given the triumphalist mood of the crowd, I did not want to shock them. One or two other statements appeared on China. That was 1999. When I left Washington in 2012, America was still trying to come out of a deep recession and the Global Financial Crisis, and had lost much of its self-confidence. China was very much on their minds. But the story did not end there.

Just in case one forgets how resilient the United States is as a country and economy, one should look at the major indices of the stock markets, which over the decade since December 2009, have gained impressively — S&P 500 +255%, Dow +251%, Nasdaq +346% by 2019.[1]

I believe it was Warren Buffett who said, "Never bet against America."

You could say the state of where we are — the great unravelling — began

---

[1] Heidi Chung and Javier E. David, "Stock Market Live Updates: S&P climbs 29% in 2019, best gain since 2013", Yahoo Finance, January 1, 2020, https://sg.finance.yahoo.com/news/stock-market-news-live-updates-december-31-2019-131332122.html

some 30 years ago. Others with climate change in mind would go further back in history. But from where I sit, as a political scientist, I see a clear acceleration of contemporary populism and nationalism in the last couple of decades. In Europe and in the United States, populist movements gained sway. Some populist parties were linked to the left. The most successful were associated with the right in both Europe and the United States. It was a different kind of politics, a new vocabulary but always filled with bitterness and anger. Large swathes of population, ordinary people, felt the system did not work for them. Their incomes stagnated, or they lost income altogether and their self-respect. Established elites found it hard to hold electoral support when many felt forgotten and left behind. Politicians spouting angry and hostile exclusionist rhetoric captured the ground.

In the United States, the election of Donald J. Trump brought onto the global stage a leader who believed in disrupting the status quo to return America and the world to what was and what it should be, through rallying calls of "America First" and "Make America Great Again". He understood and tapped into the anger of a large segment of the electorate who believe that they lost out in globalisation. In China, President Xi Jinping spelt out "The China Dream" and visions of breath-taking connectivity and technological advancement. Structurally, it could have been predicted that the United States and China would be headed into rough territory as the established power faces the rising power. Ultimately, it is about dominance in the international order.

In Asia, most of the attention has been focused on tracking the developments of the United States-China relationship, with the political elites, business community, media, intelligentsia and even the average man on the street asking if the two superpowers would end up in war. For many Asians, it is about their future.

Indeed, a great deal has happened in the last four years, with multilateral institutions weakened and uncertain on the global stage due to deliberate political decisions and withdrawal of support, while the core institutions of democracy and capitalism were being eroded and floundering, judging from what was happening in America, the beacon for so long of democratic values and of the market economy and capitalism.

So there seems to be a great deal of bewildering developments to analyse and explain. Singaporeans understand our city-state is an open country, a complex society, one which is highly connected and receptive, and would be impacted by the global trends that flow through or wash our shores. Economic ideas, innovative technologies, social media developments, political and social propositions from other places sooner or later surface in our conversations and sometimes, policies. As such, we should keep ourselves informed of the discussions and arguments and the contexts from where these trends arise. This will help us as Singaporeans to make our choices and position ourselves well.

I have entitled the series of lectures I have delivered *World in Transition: Singapore's Future.*

The three lectures are titled:

1. Disruption. Democracy Falters. Capitalism Flounders. World Order Unravels.
2. US-China Rivalry: Inevitable War or Avoidable War?
3. Singapore in a Time of Flux: Optimism from the Jaws of Gloom

The titles should be self-explanatory, but should the meaning be ambiguous, I would urge the reader to go through each essay. The third and final lecture extrapolates from these unfolding movements and tensions on the world stage to think through the outcomes for Singapore and the region.

I must say that when I thought of discussing the topic "disruption", I started writing about technological disruption and climate change. This was in early January. However, the COVID-19 pandemic suddenly erupted globally in February, having been first detected in Wuhan, China, and later spreading to Asia, then Europe and North America. The pandemic has left the world reeling from the infections and fatalities as well as coping with the profound economic effects. I had to rewrite the section on disruption. It is now all about COVID-19 and its impact.

COVID-19 also changed the experience of the IPS-Nathan Lecture Series. Due to the implementation of the circuit breaker, the dates to launch the lectures were changed. There was a short debate in April about whether to postpone the lectures till COVID-19 passed, perhaps in July, but that was unpredictable. Now looking back, we were optimistic. Fortunately, we bit the bullet and decided that we would deliver the IPS-Nathan Lectures entirely online — a first for the series — starting on June 18. I was initially reluctant having spent my life and career giving lectures to live audiences, but decided that, as I am associated with a technology and design university, I should wholeheartedly embrace technology. Since then, I have done many webinars, both international and national. In fact, any concerns with the shrinkage of audience numbers were laid to rest as the participants viewing the programme hit an all-time high for the IPS-Nathan Lectures, with overseas viewers logging in as well. There was the added bonus of Mediacorp agreeing to broadcast an edited version of the lectures as radio lectures, "like the BBC Reith Lectures," quipped Janadas. It was a first.

I would like to thank the Institute of Policy Studies for the privilege of the appointment as the S R Nathan Fellow. I knew the late former President Nathan, a man I respect and admire for his contributions to Singapore. I succeeded him in Washington as Singapore's Ambassador to the United States and fully appreciated the strength of his character as Singapore's envoy at a time when the bilateral relationship was strained by the Michael Fay episode. He was also extremely kind to me personally.

I thank Janadas Devan, Liang Kaixin and the IPS team for being so supportive throughout my preparations for the lectures and for the publication. In particular, I wish to thank Rachel Hau for being such an intelligent, responsive and diligent research assistant. It was a joy to work with her.

Finally, this publication and these thoughts would not have been possible if I were not inspired by or did not learn from my interactions with my siblings, friends and colleagues who argued with me constantly. I should also mention my younger, irreverent colleagues who brought fresh perspectives with their points of view to keep me in touch with the thinking of their generation and the generation after them.

The last sentence in this foreword is for my parents, who have both passed away, in remembrance of their love and light touch in guiding me, which allowed me to be what I am.

Chan Heng Chee
28 November 2020

ABOUT THE MODERATORS

Danny Quah is Dean and Li Ka Shing Professor in Economics at the Lee Kuan Yew School of Public Policy, National University of Singapore. Quah was previously Assistant Professor of Economics at Massachusetts Institute of Technology (MIT), and then Professor of Economics and International Development, and Director of the Saw Swee Hock Southeast Asia Centre at London School of Economics (LSE). He served as LSE's Head of Department for Economics, and Council Member on Malaysia's National Economic Advisory Council.

Joseph Chinyong Liow is Dean of the College of Humanities, Arts, and Social Sciences, Nanyang Technological University, Singapore, where he is also Tan Kah Kee Chair in Comparative and International Politics, and Research Advisor and former Dean at the S. Rajaratnam School of International Studies. He held the inaugural Lee Kuan Yew Chair in Southeast Asia Studies at the Brookings Institution, Washington DC, where he was also Senior Fellow in the Foreign Policy Program.

Bilahari Kausikan is currently Chairman of the Middle East Institute, an autonomous institute of the National University of Singapore. He spent his entire career in the Ministry of Foreign Affairs. During his 37 years in the Ministry, he served in a variety of appointments at home and abroad, including as Ambassador to the Russian Federation, Permanent Representative to the United Nations in New York, and as the Permanent Secretary to the Ministry.

ABOUT THE COVER ILLUSTRATOR

Michael Ng aka Mindflyer (b. 1964) is a self-taught visual artist based in Singapore. His practice is embedded in concepts related to flight and escapism. Using a crazy mix of interesting aeronautical forms, bright colours, a mad dose of retro sci-fi and references to Antoine de Saint-Exupery's *The Little Prince*, he attempts to make everything "fly". Some of his recent work includes commissioned artworks for Coach, Microsoft and Singapore Art Museum. Besides painting and exhibiting his work, he is the founder of the Illustration Arts Fest and also a founding member of the illustrator group OICsingapore, where he is actively involved in engaging and challenging young illustrators.

Lecture I

DISRUPTION. DEMOCRACY FALTERS. CAPITALISM FLOUNDERS. WORLD ORDER UNRAVELS.

I thank IPS for inviting me to be the seventh S R Nathan Fellow for 2020. It is a great honour to share my thoughts on an important topic with this audience. The theme of my three lectures will be "World in Transition: Singapore's Future."

Rapid change is now a constant, globally important institutions are questioned or coming apart, a lot of churn is happening, in society, in the economy, and geopolitical shifts are in the offing.

This evening I will speak on the first of three lectures I will give, "Disruption. Democracy Falters. Capitalism Flounders. World Order Unravels."

Let me begin by citing William Butler Yeats's well known poem, "The Second Coming":

> *Turning and turning in the widening gyre*
> *The falcon cannot hear the falconer;*
> *Things fall apart; the centre cannot hold;*
> *Mere anarchy is loosed upon the world,*
> *The blood-dimmed tide is loosed, and everywhere*
> *The ceremony of innocence is drowned;*

The best lack all conviction, while the worst
Are full of passionate intensity.

Surely some revelation is at hand;
Surely the Second Coming is at hand.
The Second Coming! Hardly are those words out
When a vast image out of Spiritus Mundi
Troubles my sight: somewhere in sands of the desert
A shape with lion body and the head of a man,
A gaze blank and pitiless as the sun,
Is moving its slow thighs, while all about it
Reel shadows of the indignant desert birds.
The darkness drops again; but now I know
That twenty centuries of stony sleep
Were vexed to nightmare by a rocking cradle,
And what rough beast, its hour come round at last,
Slouches towards Bethlehem to be born?

I think the poem captures the mood presented by the profound challenges we face today.

Many of us know the lines, "Things fall apart; the centre cannot hold." It is invoked so often it is now a cliché.

You may also be familiar with the last two lines of the first verse, "The best lack all conviction, while the worst / Are full of passionate intensity." The second verse and last line, less familiar, says, "And what rough beast, its hour come round at last. / Slouches towards Bethlehem to be born."

Some literary critics interpret the "rough beast" according to the era. It can be a historical force, communism, fascism, the atomic bomb, or something malignant. Is the "rough beast" today terrorism, populism, political conflict, or a pandemic?

Now that I have provided the setting, let me turn to the four big challenges the world is faced with today.

Challenge I: Disruption

The COVID-19 virus spread silently and swiftly and became a pandemic in a couple of months. Everyone in the world has been disrupted. I had completed my first draft sometime in the middle of January. I wrote about the volatile, uncertain, complex and ambiguous (VUCA) world represented by technology disruption, the future of work and the acute and chronic climate hazards. I did not include epidemics or pandemics. That was a mistake. Bill Gates in 2015 had forewarned us that the world would not be ready for the next pandemic having come out of the Ebola crisis. He said, "if anything kills over 10 million people over the next few decades it would most likely to be a highly infectious virus rather than a war. Not missiles but microbes." Gates was right. The virus epidemic that started in Wuhan became a pandemic within three months and took the world by surprise with its contagiousness, severity, and speed of its spread. Cities are in lockdown, markets in meltdown, economists believe a global recession is unavoidable. On June 17, 2020, WHO (World Health Organisation) reported 8,061,550 confirmed COVID-19 cases globally and the death toll was 440,290.

Many wise people are describing COVID-19 as a historical watershed. It is a searing experience that has touched the lives of every person in the world in a way no other threat has done before.

COVID-19 has taught us many lessons. Many things we took for granted were changed. Disruption was experienced in every domain — freedom of movement, freedom of association, freedom from fear, and anxiety for personal well-being. We fear the loss of business, our jobs; we worry about health security and food security. There are not enough masks, medicines, equipment, and we fear there will be no more food in the markets and supermarkets. Never have citizens felt more trapped whether they live in democracies or authoritarian systems.

Countries and territories in East Asia that have been successful in bringing the COVID-19 pandemic under relative control to date, e.g., China, Hong Kong, Singapore, and Taiwan, had all gone through the traumatic pandemic that was SARS (Severe Acute Respiratory Syndrome) in 2003. South Korea, another successful case, had weathered a MERS (Middle East Respiratory Syndrome) outbreak in 2015. These societies learnt and very importantly developed resilience from the earlier health disasters. Furthermore, despite having different political systems, they all share to some degree a communitarian culture where social solidarity is valued. This makes it easier for governments to implement measures in a crisis and receive a high degree of compliance. This seems to be the case too in the Nordic countries where the communitarian spirit is strong and reflected in their universalist welfare sector and corporatist economic, social model. They are managing well. But medical experts would argue it is wide-spread and early testing and a well-run and well-funded healthcare system that seem to reduce fatalities and contain the situation, socio-cultural factors aside.

The question everyone is asking is, "How will COVID-19 change the world?" There are different takes.

In an op-ed in *The Straits Times* published in April, I took the position that I do not see a great transformation happening post COVID-19. Some things will change. Some trends that are already there will be accelerated. But in the end the national DNAs of countries will assert themselves and things will settle into a new normal, a bit like the old normal. I note that Malcolm Gladwell, author of *The Tipping Point,* makes the same conclusion in a Channel 4 interview on April 28, 2020. He said the COVID-19 pandemic is too short for transformation. The Great Depression lasted 10 years, World War II (WWII) five years, the COVID-19 pandemic for two to three months. The effects on the economy will last much longer. Gladwell suggested we should never underestimate people's ability to go back to normal and return to the status quo.[1]

I was in the United States as Ambassador when SARS happened. I was there during 9/11 and for the Global Financial Crisis from 2008. Each time, there was a lengthy self-examination of the problem and the ramping up

---

[1] Channel 4 News, "'People Very Quickly Adapted to a Very Radical Disruption' — Writer Malcolm Gladwell on Coronavirus," YouTube Video, 11:33, April 28, 2020, https://youtu.be/BgydC490NG4.

of defences, a resolve to bring change — but things settled back to much like before. China banned civet cats from the market immediately after SARS, but they later reappeared with other exotic wild animals. The legacy of 9/11 is stringent airport security. Americans found they had to live with the Patriot Act, which has remained in place. Other cities in the world are vigilant against potential terrorist violence. The Financial Crisis, which was a deeply painful experience for America, is seemingly forgotten. The financial industry is more tightly regulated. The average American would say nothing much has changed in their lives, and many have gotten poorer.

Economists and business leaders predict a long and difficult road to economic recovery after COVID-19. Every sector has been touched. The International Monetary Fund (IMF) has predicted the pandemic will trigger the worst recession since the Great Depression — dwarfing the 2008 Global Financial Crisis. We will see major economic re-structuring; job losses will be painful staggering and tragic. There will be a greater awareness of pandemics for the initial few years; we will see international collaboration step-up to find a vaccine. But national competitiveness in biomedical sciences will return. Wealthier countries may increase their expenditure on the health system, improve stockpiles, poorer countries will not be able to do so. A think tank or a consultancy will come up with a Pandemic Readiness Index. Technology use will be accelerated and further developed and e-commerce will gain further ground faster. People will be more interested in working from home and want flexible working hours. Supply chains will be redirected even though that was already happening before the pandemic. The pandemic has seen a return of the state as a positive force where societies have argued for shrinking government. More than ever the pandemic has shown that decisive and active government can better deal with controlling the coronavirus outbreak. In the matter of geopolitics, we will see emerging trends accelerated, particularly in the United States-China rivalry.

I believe the importance of the human connection has been brought clearly into relief during our lockdowns and though we connect online, we need to socialise, to meet and gather. We will go to the shops. There will be pent-up demand for travel again.

Let me leave you with this thought. Over the long term, the disruption caused by technological development to the way we live, work, play and learn would be deeper and more severe than the disruption by COVID-19. Yuval Harari told Stephen Sackur in a *HARDtalk* interview (April 27, 2020) that the biggest change he sees wrought by COVID-19 is that when we look back decades later, we would see this moment as the watershed when the world accepted the use of surveillance technology in the name of health as normal and surveillance under the skin which is new.[2] This means a touch of a finger on the smartphone registers the person's body temperature and blood pressure under the skin.

Challenge II: Democracy Falters

Let me begin with a discussion on democracy because there has been a great deal of interest in this topic lately. We are hearing a steady stream of voices from the West suggesting democracy has failed and asking why it has failed.

At the end of WWII, the United States and Europe emerged the winners of the war. The Soviet Union was technically on the winning side too as one of the allies in the military alliance to defeat Germany and Japan, but it was an uneasy alliance and the iron curtain came down soon after and the Cold War officially began. The world thereafter divided into two camps — the alliance of pro-West, free market democracies and the alliance of centrally planned, command economies of the communist countries. Most of us grew up at a time when America was one of the two superpowers bestriding the world actively promoting its values.

In the fight for independence during the process of decolonisation, the strongest argument nationalists used was the right to run their own

---

[2] BBC World Service, "Yuval Noah Harari: Covid-19 — a new regime of surveillance?" *HARDtalk*, 23:00, April 27, 2020, https://www.bbc.co.uk/sounds/play/w3cszc1p

sovereign democratic governments. Colonial powers favoured players who chose the moderate constitutional path as the nationalists they would work with.

For the next 50 years after the end of WWII, democracy and communism were rival systems for the hearts and minds of the new states in various regions in the world. The collapse of the Soviet Union in 1992 for many politicians and intellectuals in Western countries was the triumph of the West, and Francis Fukuyama declared prematurely that it was the end of history.[3] It was the triumph of democracy over communism.

Today we hear a great deal about a crisis in democracy in the United States and Europe, where the systems were born and had evolved. It is not the first time that both continents have mourned for democracy. The rise of fascism in the 1930s prompted the same dark forebodings and spawned many explanations. Now a fresh slew of books has appeared — *How Democracies Die* (2018), *Democracy in Chains* (2019), *How Democracy Ends* (2018), *Rupture: The Crisis of Liberal Democracy* (2018), *Can Democracy Survive Global Capitalism?* (2018), *Democracy and its Crisis* (2017), to name a few. Then there is a rich list of publications on digital democracy — and how in the age of rapid technological change and the arrival of deep technology, technology is threatening the very principles of democracy in their applications.

Thus, the West is going through this self-examination and angst again. The question is why? What does this tell us about societies? And what lessons must Singapore be alert to with developments halfway round the world?

It used to be that the failure of democracy was associated with newly independent states in the developing world, which could not cope with the implementation of an imported system. There have been many cases of military coups overthrowing constitutional governments but returning to some form of parliamentary democracy after a period of time. And in

---

[3]   Francis Fukuyama, "The End of History?," *The National Interest*, no. 16 (1989): 3–18.

the practice of democracy there are varying models. Fareed Zakaria points to the reality that there are liberal democracies and illiberal democracies.[4]

Now there is an ongoing debate in the very countries that begat democracy, expressing dissatisfaction with the democratic system as it is practised. In a sense it speaks to the strength of the democratic system that there is the existence of a healthy discourse to find improvement. The election of Donald Trump as president of the United States, Brexit, and extreme populist politics popping up in so many countries, have raised more questions about the health of democracy, its institutions and processes, and even the very idea of liberalism itself.

Let me be clear. I am not saying Western democracy is faltering because of any single individual. The trajectory of United States politics was set before President Trump came into the picture. His election was facilitated by highly polarising debate, loss of tolerance, evaporating trust for the political system, patent inequalities, extreme allegations online, and the swirl of post-truth facts or fake facts. Brexit raises questions about referendums and party politics as well as the ability of democracies to absorb globalisation and immigration.

Pew Research Center in a poll in 2018 across 27 countries found more people dissatisfied than satisfied with the way democracy worked.[5]

What Figure 1 and Figure 2 tell us is that there is general dissatisfaction with the way democracy is working. Figure 1 shows the top 12 countries that were not satisfied with democracy, with the United States and the United Kingdom among them. The four most dissatisfied countries were Mexico, Greece, Brazil and Spain. Surprisingly, Japan is in the list.

Dissatisfaction with democracy is said to be often linked with the country's economic situation. Dissatisfaction is also linked to whether the ordinary people think the elected officials care what people think. In

---

[4] Fareed Zakaria, *The Future of Freedom* (New York: W. W. Norton & Company, 2007)

[5] David Kent, "The Countries Where People are Most Dissatisfied with How Democracy is Working," Fact Tank, Pew Research Center, May 31, 2019, https://www.pewresearch.org/fact-tank/2019/05/31/the-countries-where-people-are-most-dissatisfied-with-how-democracy-is-working/

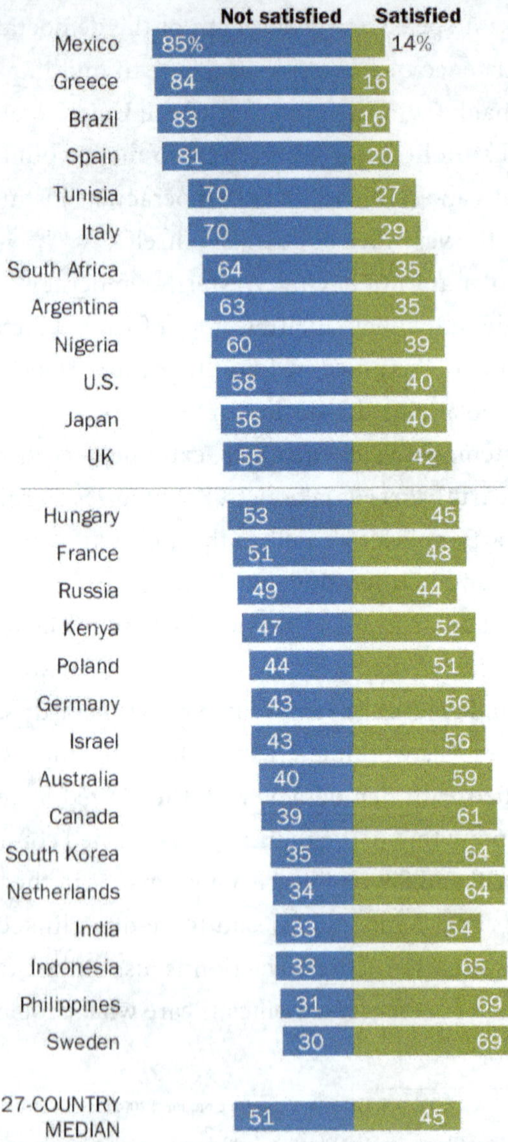

Source: *Spring 2018 Global Attitudes Survey*, Pew Research Center (cited in David Kent, "The Countries Where People Are Most Dissatisfied with How Democracy Is Working," May 31, 2019).

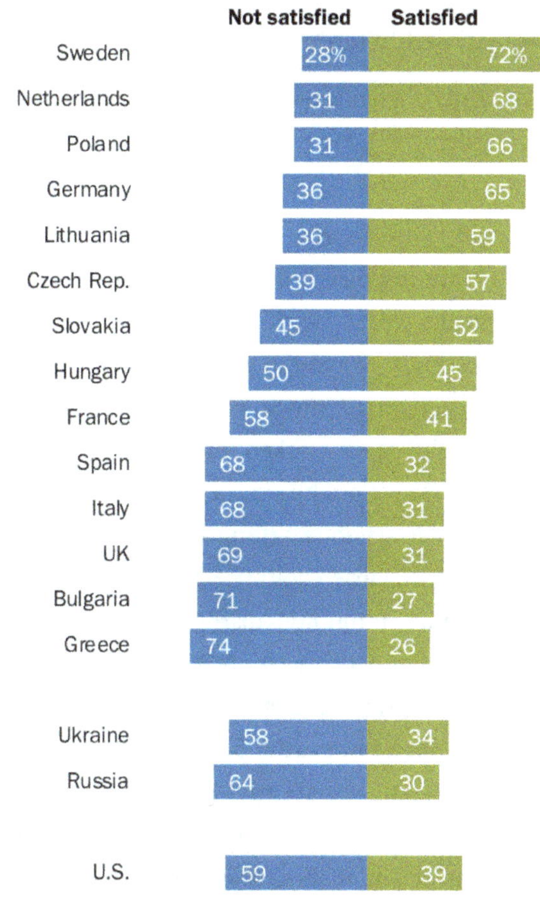

Source: *Spring 2019 Global Attitudes Survey*, Pew Research Center (cited in Richard Wike and Shannon Schumacher, "Democratic Rights Popular Globally but Commitment to Them Not Always Strong," February 27, 2020)

Greece, 84 per cent did not think officials cared, in Argentina 75 per cent, in Spain 76 per cent, and in the United States 71 per cent (Figure 3).

So what went wrong?

1. First of all, people react to forces shaping their lives and the economy.

2. Then there are country-specific narratives that affect people's perception of the political system.

There is no doubt that from the end of the 20th century, the full force of globalisation and technology left their mark on society and countries. Globalisation brought the world together, increased trade, spurred growth and speeded the movement of people across borders. But globalisation also has a dark side. There are winners and losers. Globalisation ushered in the supply chain revolution. It worked for the effective and competitive companies and the ambitious who could make connections globally, manufacturing goods, selling goods, selling services. But large numbers of workers in the older industrialised countries found their factories moving overseas and their jobs and communities disrupted. Furthermore, technology effectively increased productivity and more jobs were displaced. In fact, it has been argued that technology has displaced more jobs than globalisation.

To job anxiety, there is an added aggravation from increased migration. Many Americans apparently feel it. In Europe, the wave of refugees strained the openness towards new immigrants. Over time, the numbers look threatening and fears of loss of identity, a "us versus them" mentality took hold of a segment of the electorate. "America First" and Brexit are political responses to these issues. In European democracies, right wing anti-immigrant parties have emerged and seem to poll well.

Then there is the growing inequality in many countries. According to the Federal Reserve data in 2018, the richest 10 per cent in the United States held 70 per cent of total household wealth. In 1989 it was 60 per cent of total household wealth. The next 50th–90th percentiles received a share of 29 per cent over the same period. The bottom 50 per cent saw

Figure 3. Do Elected Officials Care about Ordinary Citizens?

Do elected officials care about
ordinary citizens?
% who ___ most elected officials care what people like
them think
Disagree Agree
U.S. 71% 27%
Canada 62 37
Greece 84 13
Bulgaria 78 17
France 76 23
Spain 76 23
Czech Rep. 73 23
Hungary 71 23
UK 70 28
Italy 68 29
Lithuania 64 28
Slovakia 63 35
Germany 62 33
Poland 48 45
Netherlands 48 51
Sweden 42 56
MEDIAN 69 28
Ukraine 80 15
Russia 58 36
Japan 73 25
Australia 63 36
South Korea 62 36
India 31 55
Philippines 29 69
Indonesia 18 67
MEDIAN 47 46
Tunisia 79 17
Lebanon 66 30
Israel 59 38
Turkey 39 55
Nigeria 66 31
Kenya 58 39
South Africa 44 50
Argentina 75 21
Brazil 67 26
Mexico 62 33
34-COUNTRY MEDIAN 64 32

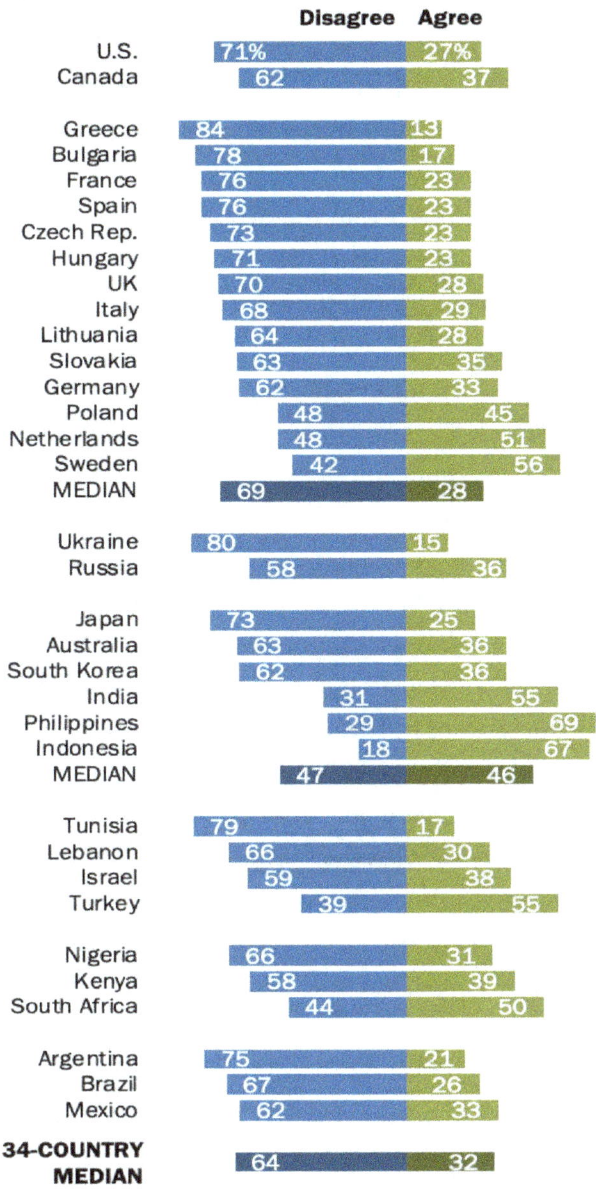

Source: Ibid.

essentially zero net gains over 30 years during which their total share of wealth went from 4 to 1 per cent.[6] This is startling in a country known to provide opportunities and hope for its people.

The wealth gap shows up in the United Kingdom as well. From April 2016 to March 2018, the top three wealth deciles held 76 per cent of all wealth in Britain, while the bottom three wealth deciles held 2 per cent. The top 10 per cent wealth share of the total wealth was 45 per cent, largely unchanged from 10 years ago.[7]

To these general trends that fuel dissatisfaction, we can add the politics of the individual countries that have given the impression that democracy has degraded. The institutions and leaders are not performing. In the United States, Congress is gridlocked. Politics is polarised. There is an inability of the Democrats and the Republicans to work together, and shutdowns of Congress are more often and last longer periods over funding bills. In the Clinton Administration, Congress shut down for 21 days in 1995–1996 over opposition to his spending cuts. The shutdown during the Obama Presidency over the Patient Protection and Affordable Care Act lasted 16 days. During the Trump Administration in 2018–2019 there was a 35-day shutdown, the longest in American history, over funding for the expansion of the United States-Mexico border barrier. A shutdown means some government services will be temporarily stopped and not be funded. Finally, the way power has been wielded by President Trump has sent American academics and commentators into overdrive in analysing him.

British politicians have left the world breathless at how the country's constitutional future was decided by a simple majority vote in a referendum and how long it took the leaders and parliament to pass the legislation on Brexit, described by British national media as bumbling and fumbling.

---

[6] Michael Batty, Jesse Bricker, Joseph Briggs, Elizabeth Holmquist, Susan McIntosh, Kevin Moore, Eric Nielsen, Sarah Reber, Molly Thatto, Kamila Sommer, Tom Sweeney, and Alice Henriques Volz, "Introducing the Distributional Financial Accounts of the United States," *Finance and Economics Discussion Series* (Washington: Board of Governors of the Federal Reserve System, 2019).

[7] Office for National Statistics, "Total Wealth in Great Britain: April 2016 to March 2018," *Total Wealth in Great Britain — Office for National Statistics*, December 5, 2019, https://www.ons.gov.uk/peoplepopulationandcommunity/personalandhouseholdfinances/incomeandwealth/bulletins/totalwealthingreatbritain/april2016tomarch2018

The fact that Brexit actually happened had some cheering that democracy had won. Meanwhile, Spain had four general elections in four years, yet parties could not form a coalition in 2019, so much so that 90 per cent of the electorate polled expressed anger at the politicians for their inability to form a government.[8][5]

Little wonder that the Edelman Trust Barometer shows that trust in government has been eroded severely. Interestingly, countries in Asia still have trust in their government and in Singapore trust level is as high as 70 per cent as Figure 4 shows. Western democracies did quite badly.

We are only beginning to appreciate the value of trust in the functioning of democracy and good government. Francis Fukuyama highlights trust as an element of social capital that help some societies to organise and prosper.[9] Here I am talking of trust in the political institutions, political processes and the political leaders, which makes negotiations and working out compromises achievable. This is necessary in a democracy and good governance. In the recession of 1984/1985 Singapore leaders managed to persuade workers to accept a cut in the Central Provident Fund (CPF) to preserve the jobs and keep investors in the country. At that time both employers and employees would contribute 25 per cent each to CPF. That is, on top of the salary given to the employee, the employer had to contribute an additional 25 per cent of the salary to the employee's CPF account. The government added that if the economy improved, the CPF cuts would be restored. CPF was gradually restored, but never up to 25 per cent. However, other benefits and opportunities kicked in when the economy grew, and people accepted it.

Much has been spoken of how social media has exponentially rendered governance more difficult. George Yeo, in the 24th Gordon Arthur Ransome Oration, eloquently described the impact of social media, which creates echo chambers fragmenting society, but also reintegrates and combines

---

8 Carlos Delclós, "Spain Has a Democratic Problem — the People Have Outgrown Its Political System," *The Guardian*, September 26, 2019.

9 Francis Fukuyama, *Trust: The Social Virtues and the Creation of Prosperity* (New York: The Free Press, 1995).

Figure 4. Trust in government increases in 15 of 26 markets

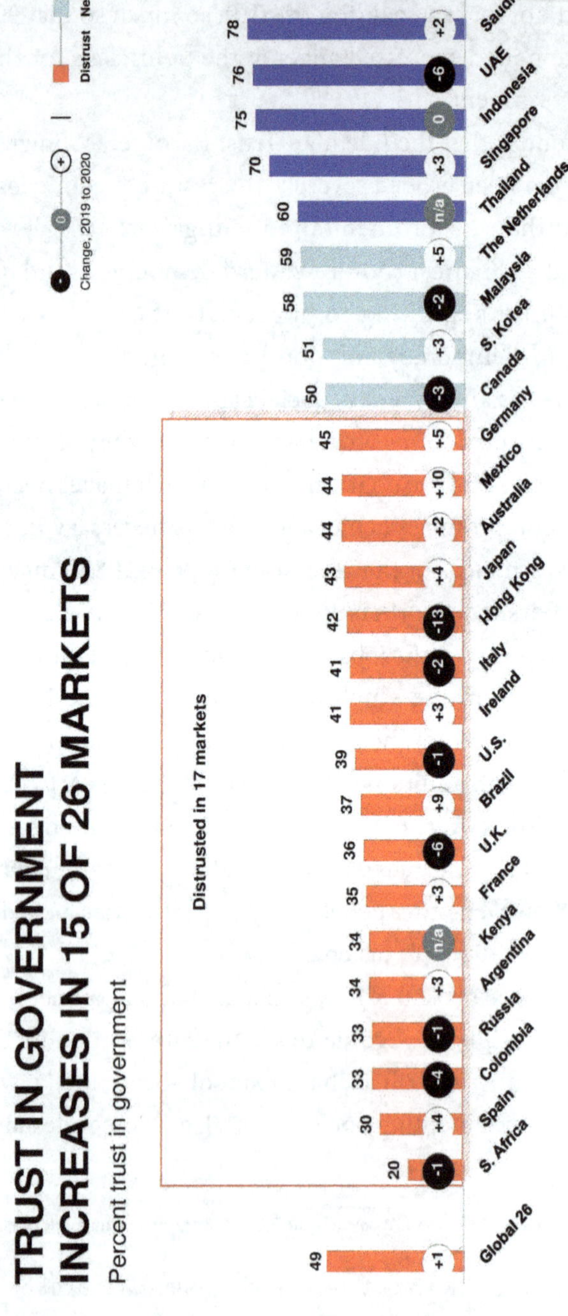

Source: Edelman Trust Barometer 2020, Edelman, January 19, 2020.

the elements into new nodes in the networks with new identities based on ethnicity and religion.[10]

It is no wonder people take to the streets to express their anger at the system — the yellow vests in Paris, protesters in Hong Kong, the young demonstrators in Iran after the Ukrainian plane was shot down. And in the United States today, there are the ongoing Black Lives Matter protests that exploded into countrywide race riots in cities, following the death of George Floyd at the hands of the police. It is a cry for justice from the judicial and law and order system for African Americans.

If democracies are faltering, can they be fixed? Some writers ask dramatically if in Western democracies the people can recognise when the system is performing at subpar and would they know the system is dying a slow death.[11] You can say the political system is not performing optimally, but my sense is that American democracy can survive any individual or any collection of people's misuse. It needs fixing. However, it is not just about changing leaders, it is reforming the process as well, which is complicated. At a Chicago Council Conference on Global Cities a few years ago, I made the point that "[t]he essence of democracy is government responsiveness to people." The statement resonated with the audience in the room. It is not the Schumpeterian idea of alternation of power between two competing parties. Power can pass between governing party and opposition and nothing changes for the people. People must know leaders are listening and responding to their greatest needs and institutions can deliver.

Challenge III: Capitalism Flounders

When Thomas Piketty published *Capital in the Twenty-First Century*[12] his book became an instant hit. It became number one on the Amazon

---

[10] George Yeo, "24th Gordon Arthur Ransome Oration: Human Solidarity in a Fragmenting World," January 18, 2020, https://www.ams.edu.sg/view-pdf.aspx?file=media%5C5215_fi_887.pdf&ofile=24th+GAR+Oration_George+Yeo.pdf

[11] David Runciman, *How Democracy Ends* (London: Profile Books, 2018); Steven Levitsky and Daniel Ziblatt, *How Democracies Die*, First edition (New York: Crown, 2018).

[12] Thomas Piketty, *Capital in the Twenty-First Century*, trans. Arthur Goldhammer (Cambridge, Massachusetts: Belknap Press of Harvard University Press, 2014).

bestseller list and was sold out in many stores. It catapulted him to rock star status. His book appeared at the right time when economists, business leaders, media commentators, politicians and most importantly workers, were beginning to question if capitalism as a model, as a system works for society and the economy.

Why so? Piketty argues that, "When the rate of return in capital exceeds the rate of growth in output and income as it did in the nineteenth century and seems likely to do so in the twenty-first, capitalism automatically generates arbitrary and unsustainable inequalities that radically undermine the meritocratic values on which democratic societies are based."[13]

The problems in the functioning of capitalism were starkly revealed in the global financial meltdown from 2008 to 2009, which started in the United States but spread elsewhere, leading to deep recession. First, globalisation which had become "hyper globalisation" saw huge flows of capital across borders accompanied by government deregulation, advocated by the liberal Washington consensus of the time, producing, as Carmen Reinhart and Kenneth Rogoff wrote, repeated international banking crises.[14]

Second, economic growth did not seem to benefit everyone and inequalities were ballooning. Occupy Wall Street (OWS), a protest against the bankers, financiers and corporates, took place in September 2011 and was joined by air pilots, postal workers and unions. President Obama felt pressed to issue a statement in October that he was working for the 99 per cent. The OWS concept spread in the United States and worldwide to Japan, Hong Kong, Seoul, and European cities on a global day of rage. It was characterised as the 99 per cent against the 1 per cent.

What went wrong with capitalism?

Branko Milanovic, Centennial Professor at the London School of Economics pointed out that capitalism has gone through three phases.

---

[13] Ibid., 1.

[14] Carmen M. Reinhart and Kenneth S. Rogoff, *This Time Is Different: Eight Centuries of Financial Folly* (Princeton, NJ: Princeton University Press, 2009).

1. First, classical capitalism of the 19th century when fortunes were made from owning not working.

2. Social democratic capitalism, which saw the growth of welfare states in Europe, starting after WWII and ending in the 1980s, softening the hard edges of capitalism.

3. Now, there is present day liberal capitalism or liberal meritocratic capitalism "where rich individuals are capital rich and labour rich."[15]

In today's liberal meritocratic capitalism, there are many professionals, executives, who draw high salaries because of their talent and expertise as well as income from financial assets. The elite is more diverse in gender and ethnicity, but this masks the fact of increasing inequality. Milanovic argues that the last 40 years have seen the growth of a semi-permanent upper class that is quite cut off from the rest of society. So the division in the society grows along with the resentment.

When Ray Dalio, the billionaire founder of hedge fund Bridgewater Associates says "Capitalism is basically not working for the majority of the people. That is the reality", you know capitalism is in trouble. He quoted a survey by the Federal Reserve that showed that 40 per cent of American adults cannot come up with US$400 in case of emergency.[16][12]

The inequalities are most acute in the United States. Europe has seen better income distribution with the Scandinavian countries and Netherlands doing much better. President Macron continues to be challenged on the streets by the "yellow vests" who began by protesting against the increase in fuel taxes and general economic conditions and demands for an increase in the minimum wage, but French writers worry about the increasing tendency towards extremism across the political

---

[15] Branko Milanovic, "The Clash of Capitalisms: The Real Fight for the Global Economy's Future," *Foreign Affairs*, January/February 2020.

[16] Catherine Clifford, "Hedge Fund Billionaire Ray Dalio: 'Capitalism Basically Is Not Working for the Majority of People,'" *CNBC*, January 16, 2019, https://www.cnbc.com/2019/01/16/bridgewaters-ray-dalio-capitalism-is-not-working-for-most-people.html

spectrum. We have entered an era of the spread of populism, and populist politics and political populism threatens the market system.

So what is the solution? Piketty came up with radical suggestions not all new — a tax rate of 80 per cent for those earning US$500,000; US$1 million and 50–60 per cent on those earning US$200,000. Then there is an annual wealth tax of 10 per cent on large fortunes and a one-time 20 per cent tax on lower levels of existing wealth. These ideas will not fly. President François Hollande tried the 75 per cent super tax and had to roll it back to 45 per cent as less tax revenue was collected because of less economic growth and capital flight.

Figure 5. Views about capitalism and socialism, by party, in the US

Democrats/Leaners	Positive view of capitalism (%)	Positive view of socialism (%)
2018	47	57
2016	56	58
2012	55	53
2010	53	53

Republicans/Leaners	Positive view of capitalism (%)	Positive view of socialism (%)
2018	71	16
2016	68	13
2012	72	23
2010	72	17

Source: Frank Newport, "Democrats More Positive About Socialism Than Capitalism," *Gallup*, August 31, 2018, https://news.gallup.com/poll/240725/democrats-positive-socialism-capitalism.aspx

Figure 6. Views about capitalism and socialism, by age, in the US

18-29	Positive view of capitalism (%)	Positive view of socialism (%)	50-64	Positive view of capitalism (%)	Positive view of socialism (%)
2018	45	51	2018	60	30
2016	57	55	2016	69	27
2012	56	49	2012	64	36
2010	68	51	2010	64	31

30-49	Positive view of capitalism (%)	Positive view of socialism (%)	65+	Positive view of capitalism (%)	Positive view of socialism (%)
2018	58	41	2018	60	28
2016	54	37	2016	63	24
2012	65	42	2012	57	26
2010	58	36	2010	54	30

Source: Ibid.

In the United States, there is talk of a return to socialism in some quarters. Expectedly, Democrats have a more positive view of socialism than Republicans (Figure 5). And younger Americans aged 18–29 in 2018 expressed a more positive view about socialism (51 per cent) than capitalism (45 per cent) (Figure 6).

Still, overall Americans aged 30 years and above, and that is the majority, are fully supportive of capitalism. Frankly, not many Americans understand what socialism really means. That may explain why Bernie Sanders, though he is 78 years old, won more support from young people than Pete Buttigeig, simply because he advocates more socialist-inspired policies.

Glenn Hubbard, Chairman of the Council of Economic Advisers under President George W. Bush, makes more modest suggestions than Piketty or Sanders. In an opinion piece in *The Economist* titled "America Needs to Fix Capitalism to Save It", he argues firmly that one of the roles for an economic system is to improve standards and to deliver prosperity widely.[17] Hubbard suggests introducing policies that provide greater opportunity for people and boost social insurance. To expand capitalism's benefits, the country should invest in community colleges, fund basic science, increase Earned Income Tax Credit (EITC), and boost the demand for labour with subsidies to employers. He also argues for more insurance support for the unemployed for longer periods. And that there should be federal intervention for wage insurance for older workers. Hubbard advocates that if workers can be compensated for unemployment, workers should be compensated if they move to a job with lower pay. Sounds like Singapore's Workfare?

The Trump presidency has not defined the problems this way. President Trump has relied on tax cuts, cutting better trade deals, reducing trade deficits to create more jobs and presumably to help redistribution. He has had some success in creating more jobs, but there is little evidence that the corporations have shared the savings from tax cuts to increase the wages of their employees. The COVID-19 pandemic has wiped out all that and claims for unemployment benefits are at a historic high.

---

[17] Glenn Hubbard, "America Needs to Fix Capitalism to Save It." Open Future Initiative, *The Economist*, October 18, 2019, https://www.economist.com/open-future/2019/10/18/america-needs-to-fix-capitalism-to-save-it

As I am speaking, many of you may think what I say of the West finds faint echoes in Singapore. We are not the same. Many of our policies have anticipated some of these problems and I intend to discuss this in my third lecture on Singapore, which examines how Singapore deals with the transitions and changing systems and structures. So I may not be as dystopian as my title suggests and you can leave the hall this evening feeling less dark.

Challenge IV: World Order Unravels

For more than 70 years, we have lived and prospered by the American-led liberal international order and a Pax Americana in the Asia Pacific. There was a predictability and a certainty about an established order. That order is changing. The rise of China and its impact is what countries in the international community are responding to. But there are other players too. India, Japan, Russia all have their interests and ambitions, and each is manifesting new assertiveness. How China behaves, how the United States behaves, and the responses of the region and the rest of the world will shape the emerging new order. We are concerned with the shape of the new world order, the values and norms that will prevail but more importantly how we reach there.

In December 1991, the United States emerged as the world's sole superpower, the hegemon leading the post-Cold War order. Many scholars in America would argue that the unipolar moment was brief. Whether the United States held to its hegemonic status globally is disputed by many who point to the fact that it needed a coalition of the willing to fight wars overseas and for the legitimation of its interventions. Its burgeoning debt became an issue for Congress, especially the Republicans, which placed restrictions on the Administration's budget expenditure, especially in defence. But in spite of two wars, in Afghanistan and Iraq, the deep financial crisis and recession, there is no doubt that the United States possesses the capability to project military power in every region of the globe. But its domestic base no longer supports unilateral wars, and they question America's global leadership role when there are many problems back home which need fixing.

There is a sense that there has been a quick unravelling of the established liberal international order in recent years. Why is this so?

Let me first take a step back to highlight an important point made by John Mearsheimer from the University of Chicago. Mearsheimer argues that the liberal international order existed only after the end of the Cold War when the United States emerged the hegemon. From WWII to the end of the Cold War, there were two bounded orders. One led by the United States with its friends and allies, the other by the Soviet Union and their friends and allies. The values of the United States bounded order included liberal values such as free market, free trade and free movement of capital, free movement of peoples, democracy and freedoms, and built multilateral institutions such as the United Nations, General Agreement on Tariffs and Trade (GATT), World Trade Organisation (WTO), the World Bank and IMF. It was an order built on strong military alliances. It was also realist and included some authoritarian regimes that were anti-communist. It excluded the Soviet Union and China. The former had its bounded order of allies and partners based on shared ideological goals and military and security objectives. Then there was an area of shared order that brought the United States and Soviet Union together as it was in the interest of both superpowers to prevent the proliferation of the nuclear powers.

It was not until the end of the Cold War and the United States' emergence as the world's hegemon that we saw the creation of the liberal international order. The West led by the United States launched a policy of promotion of democracy and human rights globally. China and Russia were included in this order and they were allowed to participate in the institutions. China's growth and rise was greatly helped by this inclusion. Presidents Clinton and Bush both worked in their administrations to have China admitted into the WTO. In fact, China has done extremely well in the liberal international order.[18]

---

[18] John J. Mearsheimer, "Bound to Fail: The Rise and Fall of the Liberal International Order," *International Security* 43, no. 4 (Spring 2019): 21–26, 42, https://doi.org/10.1162/isec_a_00342

Two developments started the unravelling of the existing order and push towards a rapid restructuring of a new order.

1. The election of Donald J. Trump as the 45th President of the United States.
2. The election of Xi Jinping as the President of the People's Republic of China.

You know the facts. President Trump advocated an "America First" and "Make America Great Again" approach in all his policies and came into office distinctly negative towards multilateralism and multilateral agreements. He pulled the United States out of Trans-Pacific Partnership (TPP), the Transatlantic Trade and Investment Partnership (TTIP), the Paris Agreement on climate change, and his administration blocked the appointment of the remaining judge to the WTO appellate body, compromising its ability to work. Trump remains ambivalent towards the North Atlantic Treaty Organisation (NATO), insisting all his allies shoulder a larger share of the defence burden, and renewed his demand as recently as 2019 and 2020 that Japan and South Korea pay more for American military presence. Japan was asked to quadruple their annual payments and South Korea to pay five times more than they do now. He has forced the renegotiation of trade agreements, the North American Free Trade Agreement (NAFTA), into the United States-Mexico-Canada Agreement (USMCA) and United States-Korea Free Trade Agreement (KORUS). He has weaponised tariffs, using them for non-trade issues on Mexico to secure their co-operation on immigration. When the largest economy in the world takes this direction, it can be destabilising for the rest. On May 19, 2020, in the midst of the coronavirus pandemic, President Trump announced the termination of its relationship with the World Health Organisation and his intention to eliminate American funding.

Fareed Zakaria in a commentary called this "hegemonic abuse". I have said in a previous article that those of us in the world order business have been blindsided. We thought it would be the rising power that would break the old order. We did not expect the established power to be the one tearing up its own rules.

President Xi Jinping came into office as a leader of a more confident China. He came in offering ambitious visions. A "China Dream" for the Chinese people and a Belt and Road Initiative for the world, accompanied by the Asian Infrastructure Investment Bank (AIIB). But it was the "Made in China 2025" blueprint that was seen as a direct threat to the United States economy and security. In combination the last three initiatives sent the message to the West that China was taking steps to reshape the existing liberal international order. The fact that it stepped up its activity in the South China Sea claims, militarising the area steadily from 2008, caused unease in the region. Although ASEAN countries and China are working on the Code of Conduct, Chinese naval ships are still actively pushing ASEAN claimants in the waters and at the start of 2020 was confronting Indonesia, a non-claimant state, over the sovereignty of waters around Jakarta's Riau Islands in the South China Sea.

The dynamics of the restructuring of the international order has been unleashed more speedily and intensely than anticipated. Chinese participants at international forums have said many times that China did not have a hand in shaping the rules and institutions of the current international order. Which is why they did not rise to the idea that Robert Zoellick put forward, that China would become a "responsible stakeholder". It is interesting that some Chinese academics make the point that China does not want to tear down the international order.[19] But it wants to make some changes to institutions reflecting the China's economic position and that of other powers that have similarly developed. There is a debate going on in China on what sort of role China would and *should* play in world affairs. The COVID-19 pandemic offered China a unique opportunity to step into the role of global leadership given the absence of the United

---

[19] Shiping Tang, "China and the Future International Order(s)," *Ethics & International Affairs* 32, no. 1 (2018): 31–43, https://doi.org/10.1017/S0892679418000084

States on this issue. Caught unprepared, the latter has been struggling with a chaotic response to the coronavirus. This has further fuelled the rivalry.

Given the direction the United States-China relationship has taken, John Mearsheimer predicts a return to two bounded orders as occurred after WWII, only this time it will be the United States and China. Mearsheimer argues that the common shared order will be the space where the economic rules are worked out.[20] At the time of writing, in June 2020, the Trump Administration looks determined to unwind the liberal international order, force a hard decoupling and return to two bounded orders. But technology and trade are not so easily separated. It was easier during the Cold War because the United States and the Soviet Union did not trade extensively. Now China and the United States have thick economic relations that ideology cannot undo. Yet the signs are that the United States is determined to force this through. Will they succeed?

Will the two bounded orders re-emerge? It depends on whether allies will line up unambiguously. The European Union would want to preserve a role for itself as a pole, and it is well known that there are differences between the United States and the European Union on major issues at this time. So there will be three poles or two and a half poles. It is not certain that China wants to confine itself to a clearly bounded order. World order is unravelling. My own sense is that the changing world order will look a lot messier before it becomes clearer. I will take you through this in greater detail in my second and third lectures.

---

[20] Mearsheimer, "Bound to Fail," 45–48.

Question-and-Answer Session
Moderated by Professor Danny Quah

Professor Danny Quah: Thank you, Professor Chan, for an amazing tour through the global landscape covering so many important themes. There are many questions for you that are coming in thick and fast, and I have worked hard to group them by themes.

One theme that has emerged is concern over democracy and our understanding of it. Part of your point on democracy is that we should not have a hallowed, rose-tinted view of it. It does not solve all our problems, and you have provided a recap about capitalism, COVID-19 and a range of things where it has failed.

Audience members have asked, is the idea of democracy really at fault, or is it just the way that it has been implemented in the world? They say, what's wrong with democracy? One thought is, democracy is the ultimate level playing field. It equalises opportunity, everyone has a shot, especially the poor.

You are right to point out that the larger Western democracies have been dismal in dealing with COVID-19; the United States and United Kingdom are at the very top of the league tables for confirmed cases and deaths. But let us not forget that smaller democracies have actually done relatively well. Singapore is one instance; New Zealand is another. So it is not that our COVID-19 experience is entirely a taint on democracy. There is pushback on maybe a too simplified view of democracy. So I would like to get your response to that before I go on to some other questions.

Professor Chan Heng Chee: Thank you very much, Danny, and I thank the audience for the questions and for challenging me. First of all, I am not against democracy. I am for democracy. I have said that the strength of democracy is that there is room for flourishing discourse. Scholars in Western countries such as the United States and Europe are examining why democracy has failed in the West. I agree with those who say democracy can be fixed. However, are the individuals that govern in democracies the ones degrading it? Can technology save it or degrade it? In the end, as Winston Churchill said, democracy is still the best system, after all else has been tried.

In fact, I argue that American democracy is strong, and despite all the criticisms that are levelled against it, I believe it will survive. The question is, do individuals impact on democracy and change it? If you get rid of certain people, does it make a difference? Do you still have to fix something else? Other factors affecting American democracy would be the increasing polarisation of views and party politics. So I am not against democracy — I am questioning its implementation. If it is a structural issue, how can that structure be fixed? I hope that puts people at ease — I think it is a good thing that democracy allows for deep, even self-reflective, discussion.

Prof. Quah: Thank you Prof. Chan for that great clarification. Let me pick up on that thread of thinking because it chimes very well, with something you said at the Chicago Council Conference on Global Cities, that the essence of democracy is government's responsiveness to people. Of course, well-functioning democracies carry that property. But someone in the audience, maybe a little mischievously, points out that non-democracies also have that feature. China is not a democracy, but the people report great trust in the government, and that trust comes from how they have seen the government respond to their wishes, such as the desire to stamp out corruption. Since non-democracies are also responsive to people, how do you view those states then?

Prof. Chan: Democracy allows for good governance, but democracy does not necessarily ensure good governance. However, if you have good governance, you can bet your sweet life that there is some degree of democracy and accountability there.

Some non-democracies do respond to people, but they have other issues as well. Human rights, for instance. I am only talking of responsiveness to people's needs. But what I am reacting to is the strong criticism found in Western democracies, that no matter who you vote in, there does not seem to be any policy change. I refer to the Schumpeterian alternation of power, where it could be a case of Tweedledum and Tweedledee where both parties are a bit alike and they are just fighting, and ultimately, you do not see much change. So, democracies must maintain responsiveness to people, but there are authoritarian systems that also do this. But there are other features that come with authoritarian government.

Prof. Quah: Members of the audience and I are trying to put together a number of things that you have said. One is the point you made at the Chicago Council Conference, about the essence of democracy being government responsiveness to people. On the other hand, in your op-ed in *The Straits Times,* you also said that you do not think COVID-19 will necessarily lead to such a great transformation. I think some people are having issues trying to put these two together because, for many observers, COVID-19 has revealed a lot of the flaws in modern society. These people are impassioned about changing the system for the better. So, they want to put together the Prof. Chan Heng Chee who says democracy is government responsiveness to people, to argue against the Prof. Chan Heng Chee who says COVID-19 might not be such a great transformation. They say, this time really is different. People are suffering so badly, they need the strong state, a crisis is a terrible thing to waste. How do we make the best use of this crisis to transform societies and governments for the better?

Prof. Chan: When I use the word great transformation, I mean a great transformation in historical terms over decades. Jared Diamond, who wrote *Guns, Germs and Steel,* called COVID-19 a bagatelle, you know, something not very important. It is not as important as nuclear war, depletion of resources, climate change, and inequality. After a while, COVID-19 will pass.

I do feel that COVID-19 hits Singapore differently. Singapore is a country that is highly dependent on trade, and will be affected by the reconfiguration of the supply chains. But when I look globally and over a long period in history, while there are a lot of people hyperventilating about great changes that are going to happen, there are also urbanologists who say, "Well, don't underestimate the difficulty of changing human behaviour." So at one level is the great transformation over years, and I am talking of that.

Now, on transformation in Singapore and not wasting a crisis, I know exactly where these questions are coming from, and I do agree that COVID-19 has highlighted issues like the situation of the foreign workers. I think that is being addressed, and it is good that it is being addressed.

But I am talking globally now. Commentators like Yuval Harari think in aeons and centuries. Also, when I look back at all the other crises, we made some changes but otherwise reverted mostly to the previous norm. So, I think we will not change our behaviour until there is a COVID-19 vaccine. But when there is a vaccine, we will travel, and things will open up much more. People are speaking of one and a half years to get the vaccine. So, let me just be conservative and push it to next year — end of next year, or middle of next year. After that, we will start changing our behaviour, back to much of what it was before. I think the economic recovery will be the hardest one for everybody globally. Will it take 10 years like the Great Depression, or will it be faster? I saw how we bounced back from the Global

Financial Crisis much quicker than we thought. We bounced back from the Asian Financial Crisis much faster than we thought. And if you look at 9/11, people got over it, you know. So, I am taking that recent historical record to guide my thinking. But I will say Singapore is different because of our geostrategic location, and because we are a trade-dependent island nation. It is really the way trade is being reconfigured that will impact on us, and I will touch on that when I come to the third lecture.

Prof. Quah: As you say, in Singapore's situation — travel, tourism, some industries that are very critical to Singapore's economy — these will be affected and there will be adjustment. But I think there is also an underlying concern among some of these questions regarding larger global changes — the change that we had been promised when we went after the top 1 per cent, the change that we had been promised after Occupy Wall Street. Why have the changes not come? I think you have given us a good set of reasons, a good set of touch points in history that change did not take place following momentous, serious events.

But perhaps we could still argue about that. When SARS happened, it was basically over in four months, if not less, and then we actually saw a sharp rise in Singapore economic activity. The Global Financial Crisis was massive on the same kind of scales we are talking about now, but it was not personal. It happened out there, with financial collateralisation, collateralised debt obligation squared, and large financial institutions. And in some ways, people abdicated on that, saying the Treasury, the financial regulator, should fix it, which it did.

This time COVID-19 is personal to a degree that none of these previous crises were. We see people around us affected, we see the rising number of cases in our community. So maybe I am a little more hopeful that there will be change, but we will have to see.

Prof. Chan: Something else is happening too. I am watching the Black Lives Matter movement, the race riots, and what is happening in the discussions on race in the United States. I really do hope it moves the needle, and that there will be changes. We will see.

Prof. Quah: Yes, we will see. What we see happening actually fits easily in the taxonomy that we are building, because America has had a long time, over 100 years since the end of the Civil War. It has had the civil rights movement in the 1960s. But racism is still a problem.

Prof. Chan: It is like the civil rights movement again. People are being awakened and it is being reflected in other societies that there is the enduring issue of racism. I think this is one of the most powerful recent issues to emerge.

And yes, COVID-19 touches on all of us. Many fell ill, and many more have, or will, lose their jobs. I think the main thing is, how we deal with this issue. We have gotten used to working from home, this cyber-physical combination, we are going into a blended city, online and offline. But it is job losses that we will really have to tackle, and the increased inequality that will come with this.

I am aware of that. But I am taking a more historical view of the larger trends, because there are different schools of thought, and some are saying digitalisation is fantastic, it is going to cause a lot of changes. The pandemic is forcing this. I was speaking to a group of European urbanologists, and I am scratching my head, "Really?" Because in our part of the world, this is not so widespread and easy. You have got to have access to the technology. So I am maybe a bit more sceptical about the possibility of great transformation.

Prof. Quah: Absolutely. We have spent a lot of time talking about democracy and effective change. But the audience is also asking questions about some of the other topics you discussed, such as world order. If I may, can I switch the focus to that?

Prof. Chan: Certainly.

Prof. Quah: When you recount John Mearsheimer's extreme realist view of the world, with two great competing powers, it appears that we are in this Thucydidean world where the great powers do what they will, the rest of us suffer what we must. I know this characterisation is oversimplifying the great challenges ahead of us. But in your view, how do the middle states generally fit into that picture, not least given that it is states like Singapore, New Zealand, Vietnam, that have been very successful in dealing with COVID-19? Should now be the time for them to take on more of global leadership, and not just leave it to the great powers?

Prof. Chan: I see that small or medium-sized states are beginning to feel they have some agency. It is a question of how much pressure they can take on. We are also seeing travel bubbles being attempted, but because of the second wave, people are exercising more caution and going back a little on the bubbles. There is talk of the trans-Tasman bubble between Australia and New Zealand, and Australia wants to bring in Fiji, but it has not been implemented yet. Now, there is a geostrategic dimension there. If these bubbles develop, airbridges develop, they can in fact, impact and develop into certain groupings that can work for themselves.

Can we, smaller countries, take leadership? I think there is leadership over different things, in different areas. And in a funny way, Singapore has enjoyed a sense of leadership. Other countries turn to Singapore for leadership in ways that surprise us. But they do look to us on how we manage the economy, how we make things so successful. I was constantly asked about this when I was in the United States, and they were absolutely surprised to find we were not a middle-sized state.

I will have tables and figures to show that Singapore has far more influence than we think. Small states can influence and specialise in specific areas. Small states can take leadership in healthcare innovation, for instance. For global leadership regarding larger security and economic issues, the big boys are fighting over that. But small states are trying to have a say too, and in my third lecture I will be talking about the different groupings that are being attempted.

Prof. Quah: Your Singapore example is a wonderful one. It points us in the direction, that the way we traditionally think, in terms of footprint, population, military size, GDP (gross domestic product) and so on, may not be the right way to think about what truly great powers are. Because knowledge, expertise, the ability to take care of your people are hugely important too.

In terms of the size of metaphorical footprint, Singapore might only have five and a half million people, but that footprint is extremely large. And maybe world order should gravitate towards that kind of an assessment, rather than the traditional one.

I want to bring into the discussion some of the other things that you have raised — inequality, in particular. You have described the angst and sense of despair that so many people have, and rightly so. If I were an American, living in the world's richest, most powerful nation, and I were one of the bottom 50 per cent, and I realise that over the last half century, my economic well-being has not improved at all, I would be upset, because that is not how a great democracy takes care of its people. There are some questions on this. The point about the 50 per cent disaffection. It is really a point about what is happening at the lower end of the income distribution. Inequality in China has risen even more than inequality in the United States, but the bottom 50 per cent in China have seen their incomes rise even faster than the incomes of the top 10 per cent in the United States, so the bottom 50 per cent has been lifted tremendously. So, is it really about inequality, or is it really about taking care of the vulnerable in society? They may not always be the same thing.

Prof. Chan: I think inequality is really a global issue. Many say, and I fully believe, that global inequality is one of the big issues of our times. And inequality is a moving goalpost. The gaps are always there, and every society has to continually work towards eliminating inequality. You may think you have done enough, but then the top rungs have moved further, and you have to move the bottom rungs as well.

It is about social mobility, not just inequality. Very many surveys show that in Asian countries, young people have hope that they can move up. You interview young people of the same age group in Europe, in America — they do not think they will do as well. So that really impacts on an individual's perception of society and the future. I think this gross inequality has really damaged American democracy, apart from the polarisation and so on. Americans now realise it, and I don't know how they are going to fix it, but they have to. Jamie Dimon, Chairman of JPMorgan Chase, came out saying that we really have to solve the inequality.

Those who have thought hard about it, like Ray Dalio, have put a lot of money in education. But I think it needs to be a much broader, larger programme. Inequality is a key issue that has an impact on democracy, and is linked to technology use too. Another issue that people have spoken about is how polarised views are on social media and 24/7 cable television. Ethnicities and identities are amplified because people read and join the same chat groups, go to the same websites. That is one way of explaining it.

Prof. Quah: And there is a vicious cycle that can be set up, because disaffection with the system makes people turn away and less willing to participate in it, blocking off the avenues for people to better themselves through the system. And what you have described touches on so many important things that we need to fix in highly unequal societies. An audience member asked a question that I think that you have addressed, which is, how do we put the populism genie back in the bottle? It has now been unleashed, and it is causing all kinds of social disruption. We need to work on the virtuous cycle.

Prof. Chan: Once a force is unleashed — we all know, we are students of social forces — they take a couple of decades before they peter out. But yes, I think you need to work on a virtuous cycle, which is about addressing the issues of economic opportunities, redistribution of jobs, of looking after those who are left behind. I think these are extremely important.

Prof. Quah: I would like to ask one more question that cuts across the four challenges you raised. It is a question about Eastern versus Western worldviews. On COVID-19 and disruptions to trade, democracy and so on, a kind of geographical statement, East and West, appears to be emerging. Where does the East-West worldview separation fit in your description of where the world stands now?

Prof. Chan: I see that there is a difference in the cultures, but I do not want to use it in the sense of two different worlds, because I do believe in global communication. To say "one world" is almost innocent and naive, but I do not want to stress the differences that much, because I do believe some values are shared.

But if you are looking at COVID-19, where do we stand now, and East-West cultures, I was reading about people questioning liberalism in the West. They say liberalism emphasises individual liberty and freedoms, and does not emphasise common good as much. And that is why liberalism is less effective in correcting inequalities and redistribution. Now, that very same emphasis on individual rights and freedoms, which is very much in the DNA of Western countries, is seen in how they react and say, "Why should I wear a mask? Why should I listen to my government telling me that I have to stay home? If I want to get COVID, I'll get COVID." I think in Asia, there is less of that. People will comply more, and I put this to a communitarian culture. But in an earlier point you said small democracies like New Zealand have done well too in handling COVID-19. I think it is partly because they are a smaller democracy. But they also have features of a communitarian awareness that is not communitarian in the Asian sense. Rather, it is a small community, you know each other, and I am sure the Maori culture impacts on it too.

Prof. Quah: Thank you for that observation to a very open-ended question. Just to add on a quick observation on New Zealand. Prime Minister Jacinda Ardern, through Facebook Live conversations like the one we are having now, did a lot to build that communitarian spirit in New Zealand. That is a very important point that we will need to reflect on going forward.

Every time I speak to you, I cannot stop because I learn so much. But we have reached the end of our time. I want to thank everyone in the audience for their attention, and for asking questions. Apologies to those whose questions I did not get to mention, but I hope you will all come back to ask questions again in the subsequent lectures in this series. Normally at this point, I would turn to the audience in the room and invite everyone to join me in thanking the speaker for the sparkling presentation and the wonderful conversation. But since this is all virtual, we do not get any immediate feedback from the audience. I will just thank you, Ambassador, Professor, my good friend Heng Chee for a delightful one and a half hours. I thank you on behalf of everyone in the audience. Thank you very much.

Lecture II

US-CHINA RIVALRY
Inevitable War or Avoidable War?

T he United States-China relationship is in a bad place today. For the United States, its relationship with China has never been easy to define. Americans have always been ambivalent about how they should regard China. Is China a partner, a competitor or an adversary? During the Cold War, China, a communist regime, was an adversary lumped together with the Soviet Union, but for much of the time, the focus was on the Soviet Union as the lead adversary. It was the other superpower in the bipolar world. China was then still considered backward and not a major industrial power. The communist world and the free world were, in John Mearsheimer's words, truly "two bounded orders".[1]

President Nixon's visit to China in 1972 was the game changer. According to Henry Kissinger, around 1969, China and the United States found strategic congruence in their international outlooks. The Sino-Soviet dispute had deepened, with China regarding the Soviet threat as an imminent one. Said Kissinger, "In the face of increasing Soviet troop concentrations and a major battle at the border of Xinjiang, on August 28 the Central Committee of the Chinese Communist Party ordered a mobilization of all Chinese military units along all of China's borders. Resumption of

---

[1] John J. Mearsheimer, "Bound to Fail: The Rise and Fall of the Liberal International Order," *International Security* 43, no. 4 (Spring 2019): 18, https://doi.org/10.1162/isec_a_00342

contact with the United States had become a strategic necessity."[2]

Even before he was elected in the 1968 Presidential election, Nixon had been feeling his way towards China. Nixon was concerned about ending the Vietnam War and the post-Vietnam security scenario. He was interested in recasting the American foreign policy approach and leadership, and he wanted to show that in the midst of a debilitating war he could pull off an opening to China to build long-term peace.[3] He probably understood that he could not end the Vietnam War without talking to the Chinese.[4] In a *Foreign Affairs* article in October 1967, Nixon wrote: "We simply cannot afford to leave China forever outside the family of nations, there to nurture its fantasies, cherish its hates and threaten its neighbours. There is no place on this small planet for a billion of its potentially most able people to live in angry isolation."[5] In fact he called for dialogue and made an appeal for reconciliation. Richard McGregor, an Australian journalist who studies China, clearly identifies Nixon as the intellectual godfather of the opening to China, where Nixon had relied on Kissinger to bring it about. The two men worked closely to plan and shape policy.[6]

The Shanghai Communiqué normalised the bilateral relationship between the United States and China, with both sides agreeing to conduct their relationship on the basis of non-aggression, non-interference, equality and mutual respect. On Taiwan, the United States acknowledged that for both sides (of the Strait) there is but one China and that Taiwan is a part of China, and reiterated its interest in a peaceful settlement.

When Deng Xiaoping set China on the Four Modernisations path in 1978, in effect overturning the central principles of the command economy, the very foundation of China's development for the previous 25 years, to

---

[2] Henry Kissinger, *On China* (New York: Penguin Press, 2011), 213.

[3] Ibid., 214.

[4] Hugh White, *The China Choice: Why America Should Share Power* (Melbourne: Black Inc., 2013).

[5] Richard M. Nixon, "Asia after Viet Nam," *Foreign Affairs*, October 1967, https://www.foreignaffairs.com/articles/asia/1967-10-01/asia-after-viet-nam

[6] Richard McGregor, *Asia's Reckoning: China, Japan, and the Fate of U.S. Power in the Pacific Century* (New York: Viking, 2017), 2.

experiment with the market economy, he multiplied the possibilities of cooperation with the United States and the West. This was seen as China opening up to the world. The path of engagement was volatile. Nonetheless, it was remarkable that for almost 40 years (1978–2017) the United States and China were in a relationship that could be described as "strategic engagement".

The United States-China relationship flourished so long as both sides could focus on checking the "hegemony" of the Soviet Union. In fact, it was not so simple. The United States had to manage the complex triangular relationship of Washington, Moscow and Beijing although it was more tilted towards China throughout the late 1970s and 1980s, as the Soviet Union was seen as the bigger threat because of its expansionist policies in Asia.[7]

The Tiananmen episode in 1989 where Chinese tanks were brought out to fire at student protestors shocked the world and caused the United States to again view China as an ideological adversary. This was followed a few months later by the fall of the Berlin Wall and revolutions in Eastern Europe that toppled the communist regimes leading, in the end, to the dissolution of the Soviet Union. Both developments ended the bipartisan consensus in America on the need to work with China.

Nonetheless, American presidents in subsequent years — George H. W. Bush, Bill Clinton and George W. Bush — continued to engage China, expending their power to cajole and persuade Congress to grant most-favoured-nation status to China, support its joining the World Trade Organisation (WTO), limit American arms sales to Taiwan, and expand trade relations with China. Barack Obama placed importance on co-operation with China to work on climate change, pandemics and other transnational issues.

Jeff Bader, the point person in the Obama White House for Asia, said the period of working with China yielded many benefits for the United States:

1. United States-China co-operation led to the containment of Soviet expansion during the Cold War and ultimately led to the collapse of the Soviet Union.

---

[7] Henry Kissinger, *Does America Need a Foreign Policy? Toward a Diplomacy for the 21st Century.* New York: Simon & Schuster, 2002.

2. The ending of hostility between the United States and China led to a long period of peaceful co-operation and bilateral non-aggression.

3. With nudging from the United States and some pressure, China joined the other nuclear powers to oppose the proliferation of weapons of mass destruction.[8]

This period also benefitted China.

First, working together, ASEAN, China and the United States put sufficient pressure on Vietnam to force its withdrawal from Cambodia and to agree to a comprehensive United Nations (UN) settlement and UN-supervised elections. For China, this outcome ended the Soviet role in Cambodia, demonstrated that the Soviet Union could not protect its ally Vietnam, and that Vietnam could not overturn a regime friendly to China in Cambodia.

Second, after normalisation of relations with the United States and joining the WTO, China grew unstoppably, adding to global growth and American prosperity at the same time.

That working relationship has come apart.

I would like to use the rest of the lecture to answer three questions:

1. Why did it come apart?
2. How far will the relationship slide?
3. Will we see an inevitable war or an avoidable war?

Why Did US-China Relations Come Apart?

Many point to the election of Donald Trump as the 45th President of the United States and Xi Jinping as President of the People's Republic of China as the inflection point of the United States-China relationship. That would be a simplistic answer.

---

[8] Jeffrey A. Bader, "U.S.-China Relations: Is It Time to End the Engagement?" *Policy Brief, Policy Brief Series on The New Geopolitics* (Brookings Institution, September 2018), https://www.brookings.edu/research/u-s-china-relations-is-it-time-to-end-the-engagement/

While the two personalities ascending on the global scene at about the same time may have affected the tone of the relationship, the real cause for the sharp deterioration in the relationship was that the United States and China had moved towards an inherent instability due to a structural phenomenon. It has arisen, explains Kevin Rudd, "because China is now of sufficient economic, military and technological 'mass' that it represents a structural challenge to long-term American dominance of the global and regional order."[9] The China challenge for America is no longer a theoretical question. In addition, this is made worse by the fact that these two countries represent radically different, political, cultural and ideological systems. Graham Allison's Thucydides Trap documents that in 12 of 16 cases where the rising power challenged the established power, war ensued.[10] It seems that the chances of conflict are most acute when the challenging power comes close in aggregate power to the established power.

Deng Xiaoping, Jiang Zemin and Hu Jintao had each used their leadership to move China along the track of strong economic growth and acquisition of military power to regain its position as a power to be respected in the region and the world, guided by Deng's dictum *"tao guang yang hui"* (韬光养晦, translated as "hide one's capabilities, keep a low profile").

President Xi Jinping followed the same course, but was different. When he took office, he launched two visions clearly and boldly. The first vision was the China Dream in 2013, actually a term or a slogan, to inspire the Chinese people to "strive to achieve the Chinese dream of great rejuvenation of the Chinese nation." The other was the Belt and Road Initiative (BRI), a breath-taking and ambitious project followed by the Asian Infrastructure Investment Bank (AIIB). Many major powers saw this not as just another economic and development project, but as a strategic challenge.

What put the United States and other countries on notice was President Xi's 19th Party Congress speech and shortly afterwards, the abolition of

---

[9] Kevin Rudd, "The Avoidable War: Reflections on U.S.-China Relations and the End of Strategic Engagement," Asia Society Policy Institute, January 21, 2019.

[10] Graham Allison, "Thucydides Trap: Are the U.S. and China Headed for War?" *The Atlantic*, September 24, 2015, https://www.theatlantic.com/international/archive/2015/09/united-states-china-war-thucydides-trap/406756/

term limits for the President and Vice-President at the Lianghui. Xi spoke of China moving "closer to centre stage" in this era. He held out that by 2035, China would be a "great modern socialist country", "a global leader in terms of composite national strength and international influence", and ready to make a contribution to the world by 2050.[11] In themselves these statements are legitimate aspirations of any major country. But the speech — following activities in the South China Sea, the BRI, and AIIB — was read by the United States and the West as China offering an alternative model and seeking predominance in the global system.

In fact, it is not just the American defence establishment, security analysts in think tanks and Congress that have taken note of the strategic competition. Chinese security intellectuals and policy elites also see it this way.

Unlike their American counterparts, Chinese analysts take the strategic competition between the United States and China as the starting point. Many see it as a structural issue, an outcome of the redistribution of power in the international system. While some write about the cooperation and competition in the relationship, competitive interdependence, a retired senior colonel, Liu Mingfu of the China National Defence University asserts in his book *Zhongguo Meng* (*The China Dream*) that United States-China conflicts are inevitable, no matter how committed China is to a peaceful rise, and that the relations might resemble a marathon wherein a face-off of the century would be seen.[12]

Professor Yan Xuetong, a respected Chinese strategic thinker from Tsinghua University, well known in international forums, bluntly recognises that the United States-China strategic completion is inevitable between the hegemon and the rising power. China has been narrowing the gap of its comprehensive national strength with that of the United States — the root cause of the growing competition. Yan believes the instability of the United States-China relationship is due to both sides pursuing a policy of "pretending to be friends".

---

[11] "Full text of Xi Jinping's report at 19th CPC National Congress," *Xinhua*, November 4, 2017, https://www.chinadaily.com.cn/china/19thcpcnationalcongress/2017-11/04/content_34115212.htm

[12] Minghao Zhao, "Is a New Cold War Inevitable? Chinese Perspectives on US-China Strategic Competition," *Chinese Journal of International Politics* 12, no. 3(2019): 377, https://doi.org/10.1093/cjip/poz010

The Trump Administration dropped that pretence. In October 2017, Vice President Mike Pence delivered a hard-hitting speech at the Hudson Institute on Chinese economic aggression and interference in American politics. Many analysts saw this as the administration declaring a new policy, drawing a new line, and likened the speech to Winston Churchill's Iron Curtain speech. This was soon followed by the release of the 2017 National Security Strategy (NSS) and the 2018 National Defence Strategy (NDS), two documents which struck the same tough stance. In the NSS Report, China was identified as a "revisionist power" seeking to "displace the United States in the Indo-Pacific region, expand the reaches of its state-driven economic model, and reorder the region in its favor."[13] The NDS 2018 clearly views China as a strategic competitor.

Let us take a moment to look at the picture of the relative power positions of the two great powers and how they stack up (see Figures 1–5).

Figure 1. Measurement of power

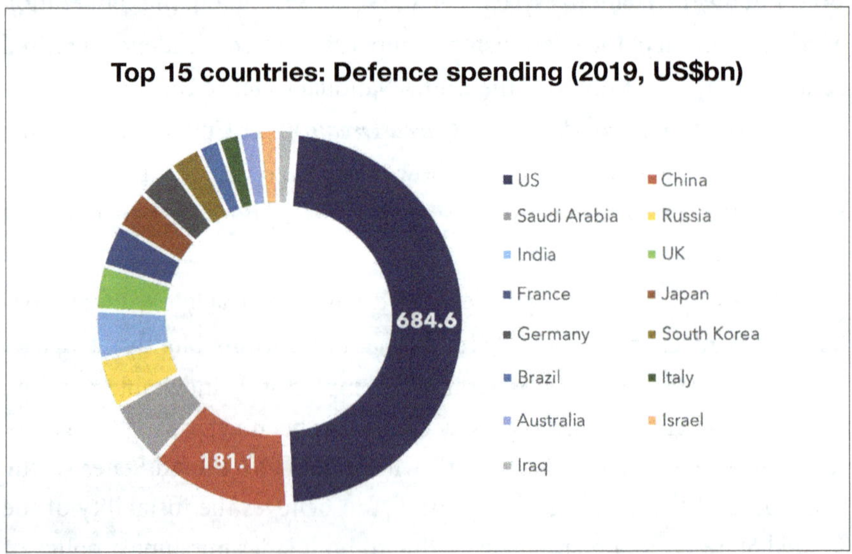

Source: Adapted from Institute of International Strategic Studies, *The Military Balance 2020* (New York: Routledge, 2020), p. 21.

---

[13] United States National Security & Defense, "National Security Strategy of the United States of America," White House, December 18, 2017, https://www.whitehouse.gov/wp-content/uploads/2017/12/NSS-Final-12-18-2017-0905-2.pdf, 25.

Figure 2. Key defence statistics 2020

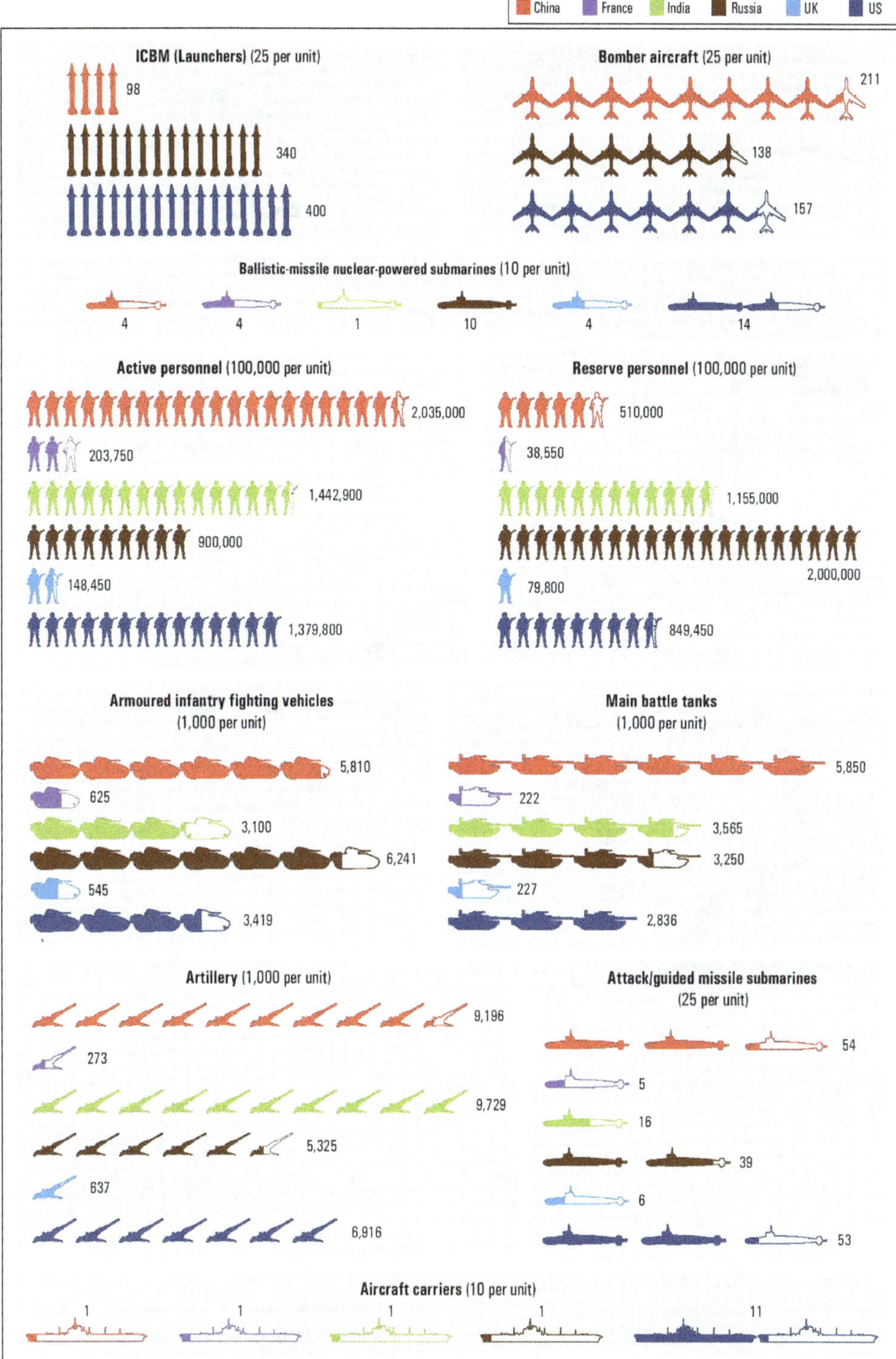

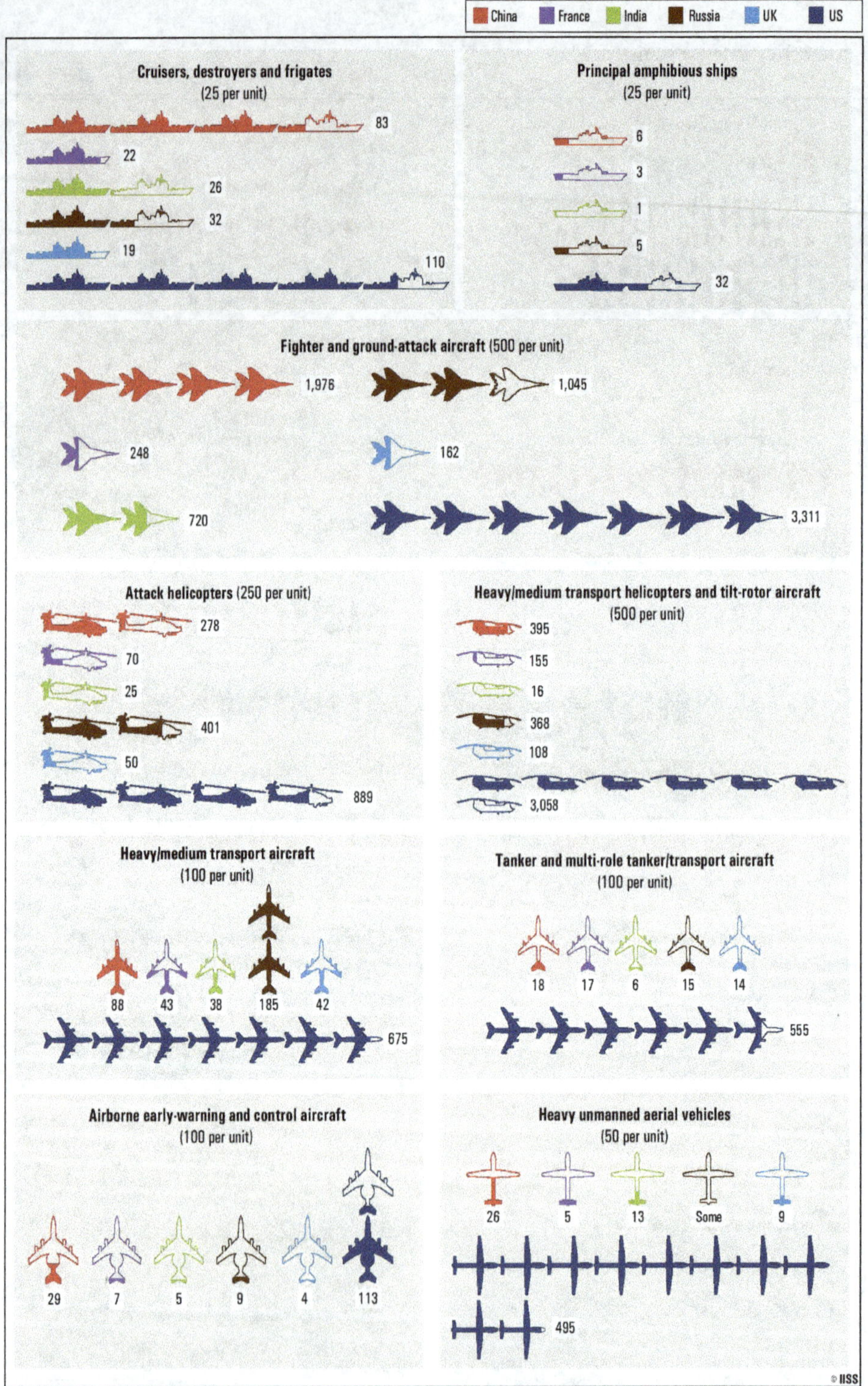

Source: © Institute of International Strategic Studies, *The Military Balance 2020* (New York: Routledge), pp. 26–27 Reprinted by permission of Informa UK Limited, trading as Taylor & Francis Group, www.tandfonline.com on behalf of The International Institute for Strategic Studies.

Figure 3. US vs China GDP figures

	United States	China
GDP (current US$), 2018 (World Bank)	20.544 trillion	13.608 trillion
GDP based on PPP, share of world (% of world), 2018 (IMF)	15.196	18.665

Source: World Bank; International Monetary Fund

Figure 4. Lowy Institute Asia Power Index, overall power rankings

LOWY INSTITUTE **ASIA POWER INDEX 2019**

Rank		Country / Territory	Score	Trend[†]	
1		United States	84.5	–	Super powers ≥ 70 points
2		China	75.9	↗	
3		Japan	42.5	–	Major powers ≥ 40 points
4		India	41.0	–	
5		Russia	35.4	↗	
6		South Korea	32.7	–	
7		Australia	31.3	–	
8		Singapore	27.9	–	
9		Malaysia	22.8	↗	
10		Thailand	20.7	↗	Middle powers ≥ 10 points
11		Indonesia	20.6	↗	
12		New Zealand	19.9	↗	
13		Vietnam	18.0	↗	
14		Taiwan*	15.9	↘	
15		Pakistan	15.3	–	
16	+1	North Korea	14.0	↗	
17	–1	Philippines	13.7	↗	
18		Bangladesh	9.7	↗	
19		Brunei	9.1	–	
20		Myanmar	8.9	↗	
21		Sri Lanka	8.5	–	Minor powers < 10 points
22		Cambodia	7.7	↗	
23	+1	Laos	6.4	↗	
24	–1	Mongolia	6.2	–	
25		Nepal	4.7	↗	

*Taiwan is included in the Index as a self-governing territory claimed by China
† Trend arrows track changes in scores greater than or equal to 0.5 or less than or equal to −0.5

Source: *Lowy Institute Asia Power Index 2019*, Lowy Institute, May 29, 2019.

Figure 5. Lowy Institute Asia Power Index, visualisation of countries' overall power rankings

Source: *Lowy Institute Asia Power Index 2019*, Lowy Institute, May 29, 2019.

Looking at the tables, it is clear the United States is still far ahead of China in military terms, but China now has a larger share of the world's economy. Using purchasing power parity exchange rates, the International Monetary Fund has given China the top spot of the world's economies and ranks the United States second and India third. According to the World Bank in 2018, the United States GDP was USD20.544 trillion, while China's GDP was USD13.608 trillion (Figure 3). America still leads in soft power though there has been an erosion in recent years because the United States itself has changed, placing Americans steadfastly first and adopting less open and generous policies towards the external world.

China expert Professor David Shambaugh says China is no match for the United States, but it is perceived to be, and perception matters.[14] It is not just the amount of money spent, but the lead that has been accumulated for years and how equipment, men, training, culture, leadership come together. There is also the fact that United States forces have been war-tested over the years, more recently in Afghanistan and Iraq, while the Chinese military has not been in a war since 1979 against Vietnam. However, what is important is that many Americans believe China is catching up fast. Speaking at an Aspen Security Forum in July 2019, Admiral Philip Davidson, Commander of the Indo-Pacific Command, said "while China's capabilities don't outnumber America's in the region for now, it's possible they could overtake the United States in the next five years."[15] There is a mood of minor hysteria in Washington these days. While the Republicans and Democrats do not agree on much, they share an anti-China hostility. They believe China's rise has come at America's expense and the United States needs to take a much tougher position with China. It is unfortunate for the United States-China relationship that the presidential election in November 2020 will make increasingly who is tougher on China an issue for the ballot box. President Trump would want to use China to shift the scrutiny away from his handling of the COVID-19 pandemic.

---

[14] David Shambaugh, *China's Future* (Cambridge, UK; Malden, MA: Polity Press, 2016).

[15] Kathy Gilsinan, "How the U.S. Could Lose a War With China," *The Atlantic*, July 25, 2019.

The Chinese themselves do not believe they are on the same level of power now as the United States. In fact, in 2019 when China hoisted in the tense mood and the increasing talk of containment — the American pushback on Chinese activity, believing that China wants to push them out of the region — the Chinese Defence Minister General Wei Fenghe surprisingly said at the Shangri-La Dialogue, before a gathering of the world's defence ministers, that China does not have the intention nor the capacity (无意也无力, or *wu yi ye wu li*) to vie for the number one position with the United States in the world.[16] China could be adjusting its rhetoric as it realises the United States is responding fiercely to smash the competition. I believe people think China is powerful, perhaps more powerful than it actually is at this point, because a great power is inherently endowed with soft power. Because of size and weight, China has soft power by being, and that amplifies all other aspects of power.

Thus, strategic competition for dominance is the most salient reason unravelling the relationship. But there is another reason.

The United States had hoped that the integration of China into the international economic system would lead to a gradual opening up of the Chinese political system, resulting in a more open society and economy. That did not happen. Instead, they watched as the new emphasis on party and ideology and the strengthening of party committees in public and private firms unfolded. This triggered disillusionment and some serious revaluation, especially in the foreign multinational corporations. The divergences in value systems as well as the operating systems of the two countries have been noted by American leaders and commentators.

In fact, quite early on, Singapore's Minister Mentor Lee Kuan Yew cautioned Graham Allison and Bob Blackwill when they interviewed him for their book. He told them, "The Chinese will want to share this century as co-equals with the United States .... Unlike other emergent countries,

---

[16] Yuen-C. Tham, "China Does Not Want to Vie for No. 1 Position: Chinese Defence Minister Wei Fenghe," *The Straits Times*, June 2, 2019, https://www.straitstimes.com/singapore/china-does-not-want-to-vie-for-number-1-position-chinese-defence-minister-wei-fenghe

China wants to be China and accepted as such, not as an honorary member of the West."[17]

How Far Will the US-China Relationship Slide?

When strategic competition and differences in value systems combine, the rift is strategic and ideological — which has led to talk of a coming second Cold War. The Trump Administration is convinced that China wants to offer an alternative model and shape a world antithetical to the values and interests of the United States. China on the other hand believes that the United States cannot accept China as a communist country and deep down wants to change China's political system. There is no strategic trust between the two powers and China believes the United States is seeking, in different ways, to contain China's rise.

Conflict in Trade, Investment and Technology

The bilateral relationship had been under constant strain over trade deficits and disputes, nuclear non-proliferation, Iran, North Korea, and human rights, but was managed within bounds. Market access was always a sore point for American companies and increasingly intellectual property protection.

Trump had long spoken out against trade deficits. In 1988 he was going after Japan. During the 2016 election campaign he called China a "currency manipulator", charged that China was "raping" the United States and said that he would "cut a better deal to help American businesses and workers compete."[18] In 2018, President Trump pushed the trade dispute into a trade war, which soon expanded into an investment war and a technology war. We are familiar now with the progression of the tariff war and the

---

[17] Graham T. Allison, Robert D. Blackwill, and Ali Wyne, "The Future of China," in *Lee Kuan Yew: The Grand Master's Insights on China, the United States, and the World,* eds. Ali Wyne, Graham T. Allison, and Robert Blackwill (Cambridge, Massachusetts: MIT Press, 2013), 3.

[18] "Trump Accuses China of 'Raping' US with Unfair Trade Policy," BBC News, May 2, 2016, https://www.bbc.com/news/election-us-2016-36185012

difficult route to the eventual Phase 1 Trade Deal. Settling that was hard and the global economy was highly sensitive to the outcome. Throughout 2018 and 2019, trade, investment and technology issues were caught up in the dynamics of the larger United States-China strategic competition, and progressively the issues moved to include ideology and values and this deepening dispute cannot be fully understood apart from these two aspects.

In the 21st century, national power, national strength and global dominance will be decided by technology. It is in the area of the technologies of the future that the United States-China strategic competition will be hardest fought and where redlines will be drawn. Technologies based on data and artificial intelligence will determine productivity, competitiveness and have an impact on national security. In fact, the two countries have been moving towards this realisation for some time. During the Obama Administration, there was increased awareness that Chinese venture capital firms sometimes with support from state-backed sources were structuring deals to bypass the Committee for Foreign Investment in the United States (CFIUS) to invest in and buy Silicon Valley technology.[19]

In announcing the "Made in China 2025" policy in 2015, China immediately put American business and government on alert and created alarm in security circles. This is a 10-year blueprint for Chinese technology self-sufficiency domestically and technology dominance internationally in the long run, funded by the state. In addition, there are other roadmaps such as the document "China's Next Generation Artificial Intelligence Development, 2017" aimed at making China the world's number one in artificial intelligence innovation by 2030.

As Hank Paulson, the former United States Secretary of Treasury, and an old friend of China, put it at the Bloomberg New Economy Forum in Singapore in 2018, for Americans, "Made in China 2025" signals that foreign firms are not needed in many areas but in the meantime, they are expected

---

[19] Paul Triolo, "US-China Competition: The Coming Decoupling?" *RSIS Commentary*, October 23, 2019, https://www.rsis.edu.sg/rsis-publication/rsis/geopolitics-and-technology-us-china-competition-the-coming-decoupling/#.X4W3-9AzY2w, 2.

to "act in ways that bolster China's indigenisation of technology, knowledge, and business processes …. It is not just that foreign technologies are being transferred and digested. It is that they are being reworked so that foreign technologies become Chinese technology through an indigenisation process that many of the multinational CEOs I talk to believe is grossly unfair to the innovators and dreamers at the heart of their companies."[20]

This technology competition will spill into a technology war. Paulson warned of an economic iron curtain that would build new walls on both sides and unmake the global economy. This would lead to decoupling. Clearly it did not dissuade anyone. Some segments of the administration and Congress are pushing for the technology containment of China.

In 2018 and 2019, the Trump Administration introduced clear measures seeking to contain China's technology rise. First, there is the passage of the United States Foreign Investment Risk Reduction Modernization Act (FIRRMA), which governs the reviews under CFIUS and then the Export Control Reform Act (ECRA). Together these two pieces of legislation expanded the range of deals the American government could review and block, and the range of technologies that would trigger a mandatory review. Second, there is a systematic review of the supply chains of the Defence Department seeking to weed out the overdependence on China-based information and communications technology (ICT) supply chains to ensure supply chain security. Third, the administration targeted Huawei as the Chinese icon, which epitomises the technology war. It has made it harder for Huawei to do business in the United States, placing the company and 68 of its affiliates on a list that American companies cannot sell to without government approval. China retaliated with its own list. The administration has since expanded the list twice, in August 2019 and May 2020, adding Chinese entities that American agencies are prohibited from using and with which American firms cannot deal. In May 2020, the

---

[20] Henry M. Paulson, Jr., "Remarks by Henry M. Paulson, Jr., on the United States and China at a Crossroads, at the Bloomberg New Economy Forum in Singapore," Paulson Institute, November 7, 2018, https://www.paulsoninstitute. org/press_release/remarks-by-henry-m-paulson-jr-on-the-united-states-and-china-at-a-crossroads/

Senate passed legislation to force Chinese companies listed on the United States Stock Exchange to delist unless they complied with American laws. The administration has further gone to its allies and partners around the world to put pressure on them to exclude Huawei in their 5G roll out. Third countries are under pressure to choose sides.

Countries are bracing for the decoupling and the emergence of two technology orders each using different standards and norms.

But there is pushback.

Reports throughout 2019 and the first quarter of 2020 suggest that American business is pushing back as the administration attempts to cut off China from access to American products. Companies that specialise in microchips, artificial intelligence, biotechnology and other industries are alarmed by attempts to restrict the flow of technology to China. This and the restrictions on Chinese investment in the United States are seen as stunting the sector's development. The tech industry is warning that limiting access to the Chinese market would cripple American companies and end up undercutting the United States as the biggest global hub of research and development (R&D) as revenues from that market fuel research innovation. To give you an idea, China accounts for 36 per cent of the revenue of United States semiconductor producers.

Moreover, a *New York Times* report suggests that foreign companies are moving away from American components and technology due to concerns that access to parts could be abruptly cut off because of policy turns. Ironically, decoupling is taking place in a different way. American companies are being driven to invest in research centres in Canada, Israel and the United Kingdom to be out of the reach of the American government. American companies share the administration's view that technology is a national security concern and needs protection, but believe the regulations are too sweeping and broad. IBM has written to the Commerce Department asking for a redraft of the policy, which they argue will lead to the disengagement of American business from global markets and suppliers. They are uncomfortable with the policy of including economic threats (or threat of competition) as a national security threat.[21] Still, on 15 May 2020, the Trump Administration moved to block global chip supplies to Huawei Technologies, which it has blacklisted. It expanded United States authority to require licences for sales to Huawei of semiconductors made with United States technology, consequently expanding its reach to halt exports to the Chinese company. A Commerce Department official explaining the policy said, "This action puts America first, American companies first and American national security first."[22] It is difficult not to conclude that the tech war is in full swing.

On the Chinese side, their companies are moving to limit or exclude American components in their supply chain. One can expect the Chinese to accelerate their plans to achieve self-sufficiency given the American threats and measures. So they too are making decoupling happen. Tech analysts, those in the business, suggest for now that a quiet continuity is going on. China remains a very attractive productive base for companies because of its trained labour, good infrastructure and dense ecosystem of supplier networks. Southeast Asia cannot replicate this. Electronic exports have risen steadily because of dense networks. China is courting companies to stay. The United States' foreign direct investment from 2010 to 2019 held steady in spite of Trump's rhetoric. In 2019, Tesla put a US$5 billion investment for its Gigafactory in China. Exxon Mobil committed to a US$10 billion complex in Guangdong in 2018. But semiconductor decoupling might happen because of American restrictions. We should watch what happens next.

I have tried to give you an idea of how the United States-China rivalry and competition has expanded from trade and national security to investment, technology and values. I would like to highlight briefly two other areas to show how the issues can broaden.

---

[21] Ana Swanson and David McCabe, "Trump Effort to Keep U.S. Tech Out of China Alarms American Firms," *The New York Times,* February 16, 2020, https://www.nytimes.com/2020/02/16/business/economy/us-china-technology.html

[22] David Shepardson, Karen Freifeld, and Alexandra Alper, "U.S. Moves to Cut Huawei off from Global Chip Suppliers as China Eyes Retaliation," *Reuters,* May 15, 2020, https://in.reuters.com/article/us-usa-huawei-tech-exclusive/u-s-moves-to-cut-huawei-off-from-global-chip-suppliers-as-china-eyes-retaliation-idINKBN22R1KC

First, not only is technology dominance an issue, the type of technology development by China has also come under criticism. Mike Pence in his 2018 speech warned that China was using the BRI to spread Chinese technologies, standards and values at the expense of American and Western values. The United States says it is uncomfortable with Chinese artificial intelligence technology for surveillance, e.g., face recognition, branding this as "techno-authoritarianism".[23]

But a Carnegie Endowment for International Peace study found that artificial intelligence surveillance technology is spreading much faster to a wider range of countries than commonly understood. Globally, 75 out of 176 countries are actively using artificial intelligence for surveillance; 64 use face recognition systems (36 are countries part of the BRI); and 52 adopt smart policing.[24] It is not just China exporting artificial intelligence surveillance technology — many companies in liberal democracies like the United States, Japan, France, the United Kingdom, Germany, Israel and South Korea also sell sophisticated surveillance technology to "unsavoury" regimes.

Second, the COVID-19 outbreak has become another platform for United States-China rivalry. Since the coronavirus outbreak late in January 2020, American and Western media have been far more interested in using the coronavirus epidemic in Wuhan to investigate and criticise China for the failures of the authoritarian system, the lack of transparency, the suppression of information, the weirdness of Chinese eating habits, rather than focusing on what was being done to tackle a major public health problem in a very difficult situation. China was demonised and its handling of the virus epidemic was reported as dystopian and chaotic. Allegations of the virus coming from Wuhan lab were made without verification. The handling of the pandemic became an opportunity to score ideological points about democracy versus authoritarianism and against China.

---

[23] U.S. Congress, Hearing on a *"World-Class" Military: Assessing China's Global Military Ambitions before the U.S.-China Economic and Security Review Commission* (116th Congress, 1st session, June 20, 2019, 113.

[24] Steven Feldstein, "The Global Expansion of AI Surveillance," Working Paper, Carnegie Endowment for International Peace, September 17, 2019, https://carnegieendowment.org/files/WP-Feldstein-AISurveillance_final1.pdf

Reports on the anti-government sentiments and citizen resistance were in my view overplayed. It was true that China was initially slow in providing information and whistle-blowers were muzzled, but the reports on the epidemic in Wuhan and Hubei province were one-sided. As COVID-19 spread around the world and countries struggled to contain the virus, it is now acknowledged grudgingly, that the Chinese actually handled their situation very well. Absent early on in the media was discussion of how countries could help each other and what multilateral action should be taken to develop protocols and cooperative actions and who would take leadership to move these initiatives. China on its part hit back. China is offering COVID-19 assistance to improve its image — a coronavirus diplomacy — and to gain soft power once its own situation was under control. There have been counter allegations that the virus may have originated from the United States. China should do this carefully. There have been criticisms of the "wolf warrior" diplomacy, which is not well received in Europe and elsewhere.

Consider the reports in 2008 on SARS (Severe Acute Respiratory Syndrome). United States-China competition had not reached its high point. The media reports were serious and more objective and internationally the global community pulled together faster.

Inevitable War or Avoidable War?

Nowhere is the strategic competition played out more keenly than in the ASEAN region. ASEAN is in a sense a swing constituency. The United States has been the hegemonic power for the last seven decades in Asia, providing a strong security and economic presence. The rise of China as an economic power has been welcomed in Southeast Asia as both an opportunity and challenge. Although there are two United States treaty allies among the 10 ASEAN member states, Thailand and the Philippines are less enduring allies for the United States, unlike Japan or South Korea, as the former were not driven by the same existential need for the treaties. In recent years, the Philippines under Duterte has rebalanced its policy pivoting to China, but it has continued to maintain American military ties — though it is ambivalent about whether to end the status of forces agreement (SOFA) with the United States. Thailand in recent years has gradually moved into the Chinese orbit. Indonesia, Malaysia, Singapore, and Brunei have been non-communist, non-aligned states, whilst Vietnam is a communist regime, and Laos and Cambodia, once socialist states, are close to China. So Southeast Asia is an area open for competition in the influence game and for the support of the ASEAN countries.

Some analysts have taken to saying that Southeast Asia has now become the site for the New Great Game with uncomfortable implications for ASEAN. The South China Sea is where the United States will directly confront China. Although the parties in the South China Sea territorial dispute are China, Taiwan and the four ASEAN claimant states — the Philippines, Malaysia, Brunei and Vietnam — the United States is very much a player in the region and regarded by the countries as the only effective counterweight to China. As the global superpower and the region's dominant power, the United States' Seventh Fleet, the Indo-Pacific Command has defended the freedom of navigation and overflight in the South China Sea, patrolled the Taiwan Strait as well as the East China Sea. China's nine-dash line claims and its increased activism in reclamations, and military build-up in the South China Sea has not only created unhappiness between China and the ASEAN claimants and anxiety in the region, it has sharply escalated the potential for conflict between the United States and China. America's navy responded with regular and robust freedom of navigation operations (FONOPS) in the region's waters. This has brought the two navies into frequent confrontation. In October 2018, the USS Decatur, an American destroyer, was caught in a near collision with a Chinese warship in the Spratly Islands. In May 2020, the USS Preble, a guided missile destroyer sailed within 12 nautical miles of Scarborough Reef to challenge the maritime claims of China. Later a second FONOPS in May was conducted within 12 miles of the Gaven and Johnson Reef in the Spratlys.

The United States and China both have joined the agreement reached in 2014 at the Western Pacific Naval Symposium to reduce the chance of incidents at sea, called the Code for Unplanned Encounters at Sea (CUES), to prevent escalation. Both sides expect encounters in the South China Sea to be the norm, but they are targeted to be below the level of provoking conflict.

Still, there is a possibility that a war could start by accident. Should that happen, one hopes what happened over the EP-3 incident in 2001 — when a United States surveillance plane off the coast of China was shot at by a Chinese plane trying to chase it away — would be replayed. The plane landed in Hainan island. Delicate diplomacy ensured during the George W. Bush Administration when the neoconservative hawks were in charge. Fortunately, wise counsel from President George H. W. Bush, Brent Scowcroft, and Colin Powell prevailed. The United States and China stared each other in the face and decided it was not worth war. In the present period, President Trump is in charge. He does not want another war, which could hurt his election prospects and the American economy. In his 2016 election campaign he promised to end wars, but he has hawkish advisers. China is of course much stronger today than it was in 2001, but it is likely President Xi, given the many internal problems of China with a weakening economy and recovery from COVID-19, may also wish to avoid war.

Could war between China and the United States break out over Taiwan? For China, Taiwan is an enduring core interest. It has always regarded the reunification of Taiwan with the mainland as something of an inevitability. Taiwan however has long links with the establishment in Congress, in State and in the Pentagon. There is also a Mutual Defence Treaty, which obligates the United States to help Taiwan in case of an attack from China. American defence allies in Asia such as Australia and Japan are bound by their defence agreements to fight alongside the United States to support Taiwan in such an attack. But in 2003, President George W. Bush sent a clear message to then Taiwan President Chen Shui-bian, who was pushing provocative tactics on the cross-strait issue, during the visit of Premier Wen Jiabao to the United States, by saying "We oppose any unilateral decision by either China or Taiwan, to change the status quo, and the comments and actions made by the leader of Taiwan indicate that he may be willing to make decisions unilaterally to change the status quo, which we oppose."[25] Drawing this line helped to stabilise cross-strait relations for a number of years. President Trump's White House has a different attitude on Taiwan, which borders on ideological and could lead to standoffs with China resulting in rash responses on both sides. In January 2020 after the Taiwan elections, a United States warship sailed through the Taiwan Strait. This was presumably a response to China sailing its latest aircraft carrier the Shandong twice through the strait before the election. The Trump Administration is openly helping Taiwan expand its diplomatic space, passing the Taiwan Allies International Protection and Enhancement Initiative (TAIPEI) Act, which strengthens the scope of United States-Taipei ties and promises to help Taiwan gain access to international organisations. In May the same year, China sailed the Liaoning with escort vessels through the Taiwan Strait.

Tsai Ing-wen at her second inauguration did not refer to the 1992 consensus in her speech and she maintained the past administrations' opposition to China using "one country two systems" to resolve the dispute with Taiwan. She said, "Cross-strait relations have reached a historical turning point. Both sides have a duty to find a way to co-exist over the long term and prevent the intensification of antagonism and differences."[26]

China is deeply suspicious that Tsai would be moving towards de jure independence. In the National People's Congress (NPC) on 23 May 2020,

---

[25] Brian Knowlton. "Bush Warns Taiwan to Keep Status Quo: China Welcomes U.S. Stance," *The New York Times*, December 10, 2003, https://www.nytimes.com/2003/12/10/news/bush-warns-taiwan-to-keep-status-quo-china-welcomes-us-stance.html

[26] Richard C. Bush, "Taiwan's President Begins Her Second Term with a Call for Unity," Blog, *Brookings Institution: Order from Chaos* (blog), May 21, 2020, https://www.brookings.edu/blog/order-from-chaos/2020/05/21/taiwans-president-begins-her-second-term-with-a-call-for-unity/

Premier Li Keqiang in his Work Report was noted to have dropped the word "peaceful" from "reunification", which is the standard reference to Taiwan. This excited speculation that China would proceed to toughen its stance on Taiwan. On the 28 May Press Conference, in reply to a question from *China Times*, a Taiwanese paper, Premier Li while reiterating that China remains committed to the One China principle and "will continue to firmly oppose Taiwan independence", also slipped in that "We will continue to show maximum sincerity and do our very utmost to promote peaceful reunification of China."[27] So the word 'peaceful' came back. But I would not read it as China changing its stance from the Work Report, but that China is signalling nothing is off the table.

The Taiwan issue bears watching.

And now there is Hong Kong. The United States government took the side of protestors with Congress passing the Hong Kong Human Rights and Democracy Act 2019. In 2020, with China's introduction of the National Security Law to cover Hong Kong, the Trump Administration said it would withdraw Hong Kong's special status, which it currently enjoys with the United States.

Whether it is the South China Sea, the Taiwan Strait or Hong Kong, neither the United States nor China want a conflict with each other for many reasons but they will push their positions to the farthest limits. For China, Taiwan and Hong Kong are core interests and they have more recently defined South China Sea as a core interest too. For the United States it is about credibility as the guarantor of security and living up to the role of the predominant regional power. The main concern of the region is a conflict or war started by accident between the two powers.

In late May 2020, in the midst of the COVID-19 pandemic, the White House put out a document titled "United States Strategic Approach to the People's Republic of China". The document reiterated the "competitive approach" the United States would be taking, not premised on an end state

---

²⁷ "Premier Li Keqiang Meets the Press: Full Transcript of Questions and Answers," *China Daily*, May 30, 2020, https://www.chinadaily.com.cn/a/202005/30/WS5ed1b75fa310a8b241159989.html

for China but recognising "the long-term strategic competition between our two systems."[28] The document held out promise of co-operation, but was tough on the Chinese Communist Party and on specific Chinese behaviour the United States considered egregious, declaring they would have a "tolerance for greater friction in the bilateral relationship".

It is expected that middle-sized and smaller countries will find themselves pressured by both sides to make choices in this contestation. I will take this very important question up in my third and final lecture analysing the delicate path Singapore and the region are taking.

---

[28] United States National Security Council, "United States Strategic Approach to the People's Republic of China," White House, May 26, 2020, https://www.whitehouse.gov/wp-content/uploads/2020/05/U.S.-Strategic-Approach-to-The-Peoples-Republic-of-China-Report-5.20.20.pdf

Question-and-Answer Session
Moderated by Professor Joseph Liow

Professor Joseph Liow: What we have heard is a characteristically eloquent and thought-provoking lecture from Professor Chan Heng Chee. She has given us much food for thought. I was particularly appreciative of the fact that she set the Sino-US relationship in its historical context, and we need to bear that in mind to understand what is happening now in this bilateral relationship.

There has been a whole series of questions that has been sent in and we are constrained by time, so I will try to accommodate as many as possible and group them as well. But if there are any questions that do not get answered or conveyed, please accept my apologies in advance.

But let me fire off the first question. Prof. Chan, in your time as Singapore's Ambassador to the United States (1996–2012), that period covered the Clinton, George W. Bush (Bush 43) and Obama presidencies, which also overlapped with the terms of Jiang Zemin, Hu Jintao and a little bit of Xi Jinping as well. In other words, you must have accumulated a wealth of observations following the dynamics so closely from a prized ringside seat. I wonder if you could share some of your views and observations about how that relationship has developed up to this point, from that vantage?

Professor Chan Heng Chee: I am going to try to be brief so we can take in more questions, but it is hard to be brief on this.

I arrived in the United States in 1996, Jiang Zemin made his first visit in 1997, and it had been a hiatus of 12 years before a Chinese president came to the United States. Bear in mind that in 1997, China was not what China is today. Jiang Zemin came to the United States and he wanted a good visit. It was important for him that he looked that he could get on with the United States, and that he was an important player that the United States would respect on the world stage. This was a time when Chen Shui-bian was around, so the Taiwan Strait was an issue.

In the end, Jiang Zemin came and charmed everybody, because he had a sense of humour. The visit went well and he found that the United States had not changed its position on Taiwan — that was his main concern. And during the Bush 43 period, as I pointed out in my lecture, there was initially difficulty between China and the United States over EP-3[29], because the American administration had a team of hawks. But the almost-near war or near conflict so early in Bush's term because of EP-3 made everybody sober up, and the United States-China relationship was very good after that.

Let me point out that at any time, the relationship between the United States and China is one of competition, cooperation and differences in views. The United States has learned to manage that quite well and China is learning to deal with the United States. In fact, I got the sense that the Chinese rather liked Republican administrations. But when I talked to American diplomats, they've worked out a relationship with China. In the beginning, a United States administration would be bashing China, and then they would settle down to a familiar path. As one diplomat said, "If we are going to end in this position, why don't we start at the position we will end at, rather than start from somewhere else? Because every president seems to start the term fighting with China, be at odds with China, and then they come round and settle into a relationship with China." So, that

---

[29] In April 2001, a US Navy EP-3 surveillance plane collided with a Chinese F-8 fighter jet in the airspace above China's claimed 200-mile Exclusive Economic Zone (EEZ).

is the background, competition, cooperation, you begin being tough and then you learn to deal with China.

But China in 1997, during Jiang Zemin's visit, was not yet the China that has grown to be what it is today. China only entered the WTO in 2001, so it was different. When Xi Jinping came to Washington, and this was in 2012, January or February — I left in July — I attended a lunch. I walked into a hall and a United States official whispered to me, "You see this hall?" It was filled with people, packed. He said, "You know it is a rising power." So that was the sense. But the relationship has really deteriorated.

Prof. Liow: Thank you for your answer. We have a tonne of questions on Singapore and what Singapore needs to do, but you have a lecture[30] based on that, so maybe we will set those questions aside for now.

There is a set of questions on the international order, so let me break the questions down into digestible parts. Basically there is interest in whether China does or does not really want to lead — I think you alluded to that when you talked about the Chinese Defence Minister's comments in Singapore. So, do we take that at face value or is China covering up intentions to play a more active role? That is one question.

The second is, why don't we let China lead, so that it will have a stake in stability?

Third, why did the United States and Western countries think that integrating China into the liberal international order would change China's politics?

Prof. Chan: To the question, on whether China is trying to be something else but will show its hand later, you will note that throughout my lecture I say "for now". The picture is "for now", because China is a country that is growing, changing — and positions change, strengths change, they shift. This applies to the United States and all the other countries too. But

---

[30] Prof. Chan's third lecture, titled "Singapore in a Time of Flux: Optimism from the Jaws of Gloom" was delivered on 15 July 2020. It looked at questions of Singapore's economy, societal challenges and governance.

for now, I think China feels that it is not in the position to challenge the United States.

Why don't we let China lead? There are two reasons. It is not that no one is letting China lead. Leadership means you are a stakeholder, and you have to take on responsibilities. That could be shoring things up, supporting situations. I am not sure China wants that role. They did not want to be a stakeholder when Bob Zoellick offered them the role of responsible stakeholder.[31] Perhaps they did not share in that worldview, that is one. But also, would they want to carry the burden of being the part-time global gendarme or policeman to help deal with disasters and conflicts? So, I would say, the question is, does China want to lead in that way? I am sure China wants to lead when it is ready and in a manner it wants to.

I think it is also very difficult for a power which has been predominant for so many years and has been a hegemon — so its values, its policies become acceptable to the rest of the world — to give way, to give up its position and let another country lead. And I have noticed, the United States gets a bit touchy when Europe or Japan tries to take the lead — and these are allies. So it is very hard, from a predominant position, to just allow another power to come in to lead. Which is why the adjustment in this redistribution of power is greatest for the United States. But China feels that at this moment, it does not want to take that kind of primary leadership role, because it would have to be prepared to underwrite the security in different parts of the world and enter into conflicts and so on.

Prof. Liow: There is also the question, essentially about values. Why did the United States and Western countries think that the liberal international order and free trade would change the political systems of China?

---

[31] Then US Deputy Secretary of State Robert Zoellick had said, "We need to urge China to become a responsible stakeholder in [the international] system. China has a responsibility to strengthen the international system that has enabled its success." in remarks to the National Committee on US-China Relations, which he delivered in New York City on September 21, 2005 (https://2001-2009.state.gov/s/d/former/zoellick/rem/53682.htm).

Prof. Chan: This is Western liberal thought, that when countries and societies get wealthier, there is economic development, they will change and become more open. People will all want a certain kind of political system that is open and democratic. This is the belief. The United States and Europe thought that by bringing China into the WTO, allowing it to expand, being part of the liberal order, China would change. But as Lee Kuan Yew said, China is not going to be an honorary Western gentleman.

We underestimate the difficulty in changing values. The United States is a country that is messianic, it wants to change other countries — democracy is wonderful, they believe in it and they will try to promote it.

In a way, China is not messianic, it does not want to promote values that way. That is why as an alternative model, China is not going to go around the world selling the Chinese model. As Prime Minister Lee Hsien Loong said, America is a young country that thinks every country should be like them, and they would like to sell you their values. China is an old country and thinks no other country can be like them, so they are not going to go round selling their values in that sense.

That is why I read the 19th Party Congress speech as China asserting the position to the world and in particular to the United States, that theirs is the right system: the Chinese system has brought hundreds of millions of people out of poverty, so do not try to change me, do not try to change my system. And if there are others who want to use this system, fine.

Prof. Liow: Yeah, we get the impression that on the United States side, their values are very entrenched in the political psyche of the nation. Now, there is an important question about the rivalry and risk. Under what circumstances would you see both the United States and China wanting to do more to reduce their areas of contention and increase their areas of cooperation?

Prof. Chan: Everything is possible in the United States. You get the political right, and there are the moderates and progressives — two sides.

I think both see that they do have some interests that are congruent. The question is whether when you have different presidents, they may reach for different objectives. All American presidents before the present president have worked with China to some degree. Now China has to give some, it is giving some now, opening up its markets and so on — they should have done that earlier, frankly — and I think there could be some areas where they could work together with the United States. For instance, I have been reading the writings of potential policymakers in the next administration. They will be tough with China but they also emphasise the areas that they can work with China on — largely climate change, now you can add pandemics, and there are transnational issues, drugs and so on, trafficking. I think there would be presidents that would work that way.

One of the things I recognise, having lived in America for so many years, is that America is a country that changes — that is its strength. It renews itself. If you do not like it, wait for the change.

The pendulum swings; if it goes to an extreme, it swings back to the other side. And I have been wondering, watching what is happening, whether we are beginning to see the start of another change. I have been toying with this idea. Because now you are seeing this push against racism, you are seeing the courts emphasise that LGBTQ (lesbian, gay, bisexual, transgender and queer) is part of civil rights, it can be put under the Civil Rights Act. So, I think something is happening in the United States. And I am asking myself, has neo-conservatism run its course, has right-wing conservatism run its course?

When I say "run its course" I do not mean it completely disappears, but that a different thinking is coming in. We saw that happen before — counterculture, the Vietnam war, anti-war, that period ushered in the conservatives and the neoconservatives afterwards, and now we seem to see a swing, slowly. It will not happen next year, but you are moving towards that.

So in the thinking on China, something could happen, but the rivalry between the United States and China is deep and will be there, because the United States does not want to be number two, it has always been number one in recent history, so it will find it very hard to adjust. They will compete but does the competition have to result in war? I think they could work together on other areas.

Prof. Liow: Yeah, as you mentioned at the beginning it is very much a structural phenomenon at work. But Prof. Chan, you have left the door ajar, so I have to ask you, will we see a pendulum swing in November this year?

Prof. Chan: We are still many months from the election and in the United States, that is like a lifetime. In fact, for the presidential elections nothing really happens till after summer, in September. Then you start to look at what happens. I would not count President Donald Trump out. Right now the numbers do not look good for him, but anything can happen.

Prof. Liow: That is true. We have a question on the decoupling. Who do you think will be the ultimate winner if there is a full decoupling of United States-China relations? It seems that the United States has more to lose as China always has its large domestic market to fall back on, if the United States is closed off to them.

Prof. Chan: When you say full decoupling, is it decoupling in economics, or security, or every other sphere? I just do not see that happening. But if that happens, because of the size of China, I think, it could be in fact, split regions. Let me just leave it at that.

Prof. Liow: Your point about split regions nicely segues into another question. How do the United States allies like Australia, the United Kingdom and Japan, figure in this bilateral standoff and tension, particularly given the initial support for China's economic overtures?

Prof. Chan: The irony is that many of its allies in Asia have China as their number one trading partner. Their economies are very closely tied up with China. China is Australia's number one trading partner, Japan's,

South Korea's, even Taiwan's. So how do they square? Right now, I think most of them are choosing to be with the United States on security, but on economics, it is with China. They are wondering when China or the United States will say, you cannot have a foot in each camp. You cannot have security with the United States and economics with China, you have to come on the same side. When that happens, how do people choose?

But even as you mentioned these countries, how would Australia choose, how would Japan choose — these countries have different leaderships, different parties, the mood changes, they can change the direction. So right now, some leaderships of certain countries may take the country one way, but a change of party could take the country another way. And I would argue that all the countries in the region, all of America's allies in the region, would like to keep things as they are — that they can carry on with China as a trading partner, with their economies tied up with China, although they talk now of diversifying. They are still very much reliant on China, which has a growth story right now, that they are the first country to come out of COVID-19. China's economic partners would like to carry on with that, and they hope that it would be the case. Even with Europe, China is the biggest market, how do you leave out your biggest market? So economics will lead to many decisions.

Prof. Liow: And this is where we see the difference between the so-called old Cold War and what we are facing today, the economic dimension. A question on ASEAN — will ASEAN be able to put together a united front, to address rising Chinese influence in the Indo-Pacific region? What are some issues that ASEAN would have to overcome before being able to do that?

Prof. Chan: Well, ASEAN is made up of 10 countries, each with a different strategic perspective and foreign policy outlook. They have varying outlooks. And it has been, frankly, not easy to achieve ASEAN unity. It is always a challenge. But we manage to come through when it comes to a statement. There are structural reasons explaining this — ASEAN was created as a regional organisation that does not seek the kind of integration that the European Union (EU) does. It is a project of cooperation. ASEAN has become much more integrated in many areas, such as economics, and we are trying to work out security, but we have no pretence of coming up with a common foreign policy. We have our own defence policies. So because of that, whilst ASEAN countries all know that we should stick together so that we can deal with the larger powers, the great powers, it is a difficult exercise. Yet, if we do not have ASEAN, we would have to recreate an ASEAN.

Prof. Liow: We have a question that is quite lengthy and partly linked to Singapore, but I think it is worth me reading it and you thinking about it. If in Singapore we are asked to choose between the United States and China, what should we look at in how the United States has treated China that should make us trust America? So the question is of trusting the United States. And there are some examples of how the United States has shifted the goalposts on China. The main point is, if the United States has constantly shifted goalposts for China over the last decade and a half, for other states, not just Singapore, can we trust America?

Prof. Chan: Unless I have the examples, I do not know what the audience member means by changing the goalpost. But I would say there are a few enduring principles that the United States holds dear that you can look at. First, democracy; second, security; and third, maintaining the liberal world order that the United States has led over the last 70 years — an order which is anti-communist, and led by the United States and the Western allies.

Now, are you part of that, or are you not part of that? They believe in democracy, they believe in human rights, but the goalposts can change sometimes, as with any great power. Even China, will react in this way too.

What is the major issue you are confronting at that time? China will call it a principle contradiction. If that is the issue, then you adjust some of your principles on democracy and human rights and you work with some of the countries that you otherwise would not, or under your principles, should not work with.

Security allows you to be a little elastic on whom you choose as partners, but, in other cases, they will come out very strongly on human rights and democracy. And analysts and countries have always felt that if you are strategically important to the United States, because you are a country that has oil or you are located somewhere where there is great competition between China and the United States, you will be given some leeway. But if you are a country that is tucked in a corner, small, with no resources, then they will be really tough on you when it comes to human rights, democracy and so on. So does the United States change goalposts? Yes. But I think they have these principles as constants.

Prof. Liow: Let us move on to the next one, which is a bit technical. Given that the China-Central and Eastern Europe Investment Cooperation Fund and the Belt and Road Initiative (BRI) have the potential to box the United States out of future international deals, how do you think this might impact confidence levels in the United States, the US dollar, and the future of global trade and investment opportunities?

Prof. Chan: This China-European Union investment fund, how big is it? And can you box the United States out of future deals? First, the United States can always join in; it decided not to join. In politics everything is possible. At another stage, the United States might say why not, although I think it will not. But I do not think it will box the United States out of future deals, because I do not think it will be so all-encompassing that there is no room for another player.

Prof. Liow: Could it be that the United States and in some cases, the rest of the world, seriously underestimated the rapid rise of China? How did China's WTO accession help China rise to what it is today?

Prof. Chan: Yes, the United States, and probably all of us, underestimated China's rise. Napoleon did not. Napoleon said, "China is a sleeping lion. Let her sleep for when she wakes she will shake the world." And I think he is right. I think it is numbers, it is the size and the weight of China, the ingenuity and the creativity. They are very smart people. The Chinese have done very well by WTO. All of us have done well, frankly. The moment countries open up their economies and move into the international realm, you join the international system, open economies, and your economy will take off. And that was what persuaded a lot of countries in Southeast Asia to open up, adopt export-oriented strategies, move away from import substitution, join the world. For a long time we were trying to persuade Myanmar to do the same. In China, they opened up, joined WTO, did all the right things, and China is a huge market. It is not just what China is doing outside. China is a market, so I think it is very attractive to all the investors. So we should not have been surprised.

Prof. Liow: We have time for one final question. There are some arguments in China that the technological decoupling would change the Chinese economy's focus to innovation-centred development and emphasise Chinese techno-nationalism. Do you see this happening?

Prof. Chan: China is trying to be self-sufficient now, because they are forced to do so, and they will do it very rapidly. Is that techno-nationalism? Every country is getting more nationalistic and I think the United States is also showing some techno-nationalism about their technology. If China succeeds in achieving everything they want, they will be very proud of it, they will be very nationalistic about it. How will they deal — will they be generous? How will they share the technology? That will be interesting to watch. There needs to be some discussion about how we use technology, how we regulate artificial intelligence globally. Would all the countries — China, United States, every other country — come together and talk about common standards? At some stage, we will have to discuss this. How you are going to run a world on split standards? And if being techno-nationalist means you are a world onto yourself and you do not want to talk with others and discuss standards and norms, how are you going to export your technology? If it is going to be exportable, then there has to be some discussion.

Prof. Liow: I have to bring the Q&A session to a close, because we are really running short of time. I really look forward to listening to Prof. Chan's lectures because you learn so much within a short period of time. And again, I have not been disappointed. So, thank you very much, Prof. Chan, it was a tour de force not only on Sino-US relations, but really on the broader canvas on which the portrait of this bilateral relationship is being painted. And the subtext to your lecture also makes a point — just as China and the United States are shaping the world, they are also being shaped by the larger developments, as is their bilateral relationship. I think this segues nicely into the question on how we in Singapore, can, should, must, position ourselves in relation to these dynamics. But that is a topic not for tonight, that is for your next lecture, which I encourage everyone to take note of — it happens after the election, so no excuse. Until the next lecture, it leaves me to thank you on behalf of our virtual audience, Prof. Chan, for a very fantastic, illuminating lecture. Thank you very much.

Lecture III

SINGAPORE IN A TIME OF FLUX
Optimism from the Jaws of Gloom

The Singapore General Election 2020 (GE2020) is over. The People's Action Party (PAP) government has been returned to office with 61.24 per cent of the vote and 83 of the 93 seats. The Workers' Party now holds two Group Representation Constituencies (GRCs) and a Single Member Constituency (SMC), 10 seats in all, and for the first time since independence Singapore has a Leader of the Opposition in Parliament (Figure 1). This is a historic watershed. The election demonstrated that the electorate chose safety, security and solutions by returning the incumbent PAP to power but at the same time wanted to strengthen opposition voices and checks and balance in the legislature.

There have been so many intelligent and sharp analyses in social media post-election that I do not want to go over the same ground. Let me make a few observations about trends that point to what sort of politics we will have in the future.

The electoral result was a vote on the last five years, the last five months and the last nine days. Let me explain. The last five years: Voters were looking at PAP predominance or the "supermajority" and how governance and parliamentary debate had been conducted. They did not approve of the

Figure 1. Map showing results of the 2020 General Election

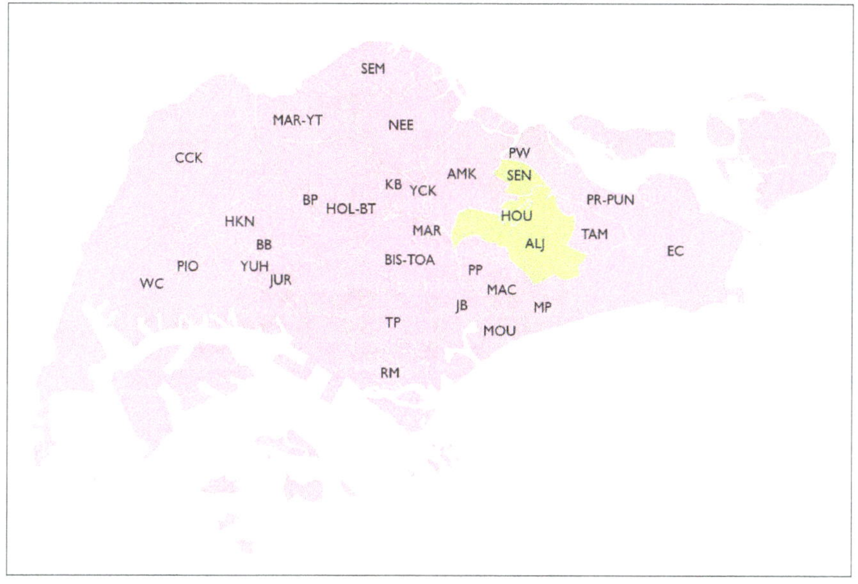

Source: Cai Dewei for the Institute of Policy Studies

way the Elected President was introduced and other policies as well, like the Protection from Online Falsehoods and Manipulation Act (POFMA). Last five months: The vote was also on how the COVID-19 pandemic was handled with the lack of clarity and micromanaging of rules and protocols for businesses. There were also growing fears and anxieties about jobs. In the last nine days of the campaign, it was about messaging, communicating, and the online presence and savviness of the parties.

Which brings me to an important fact and trend in our society. We talk a great deal about the youth vote and younger voters. Let me show you our demographic bulge represented in Figure 2. What has not been highlighted in the commentaries is that the GE2020 occurs at a time when Singapore is at its youth peak. Thereafter the younger cohorts are shrinking. There is a sizeable population bulge, aged between 25 and 44; and if you include those aged 20 to 24, it is a huge group. The Workers' Party understood this and chose youthful candidates and issues for the Zoomer generation who prefer personal narratives and "I feel your pain"

Figure 2. Age pyramid of Singapore's resident population (as of June 2019)

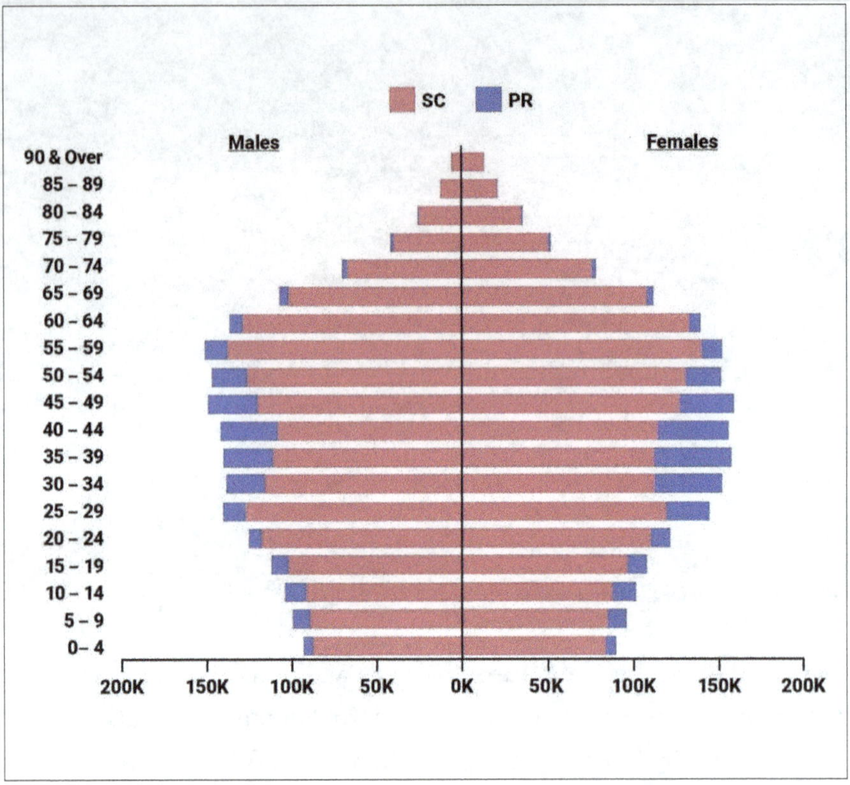

Source: *Population in Brief 2019* (Singapore: National Population & Talent Division, Strategy Group, Prime Minister's Office, September 2019)

connectivity, approachability, and authenticity. This online digital politics is the new retail politics — up close and personal.

Clearly, this age group bought the opposition message of the need for diverse voices in Parliament and the need for checks and balances. The question is, as this demographic group grows older, will their values and issues change? It has been conventional wisdom that as people get older they become more conservative, but a Pew Research report suggests that American millennials and Gen Xers are different from Baby Boomers and the silent older generation (labelled the "Silents" in Pew's report). They buck the trend of changing and on many issues they have a distinct and increasingly liberal outlook.[1] So I expect our millennials will continue to support diverse voices and an opposition in Parliament as a good thing even as they age. They will have specific personal concerns too in different phases of their lives. The incumbent party will have to understand this group better to win back their vote.

During the campaign and in the post-GE2020 analysis, the word that comes up in most conversations is "fair". There is a strong desire to see the incumbents play politics more fairly when dealing with the opposition. I have been thinking about the evolving political culture of Singapore for some time now. As I listen to panellists and read the online posts, it is evident that a new Singapore political culture is emerging. On the one hand is the culture of government, which emphasises strong government, effectiveness, a legalistic culture, delivery of public goods and services, and a better life for the people. Critics have characterised the PAP political style as paternalistic. On the other hand, many Singaporeans invoke democracy and want to see Singapore evolve into a full-fledged democracy. Yet political commentators have asked why the PAP is asking for a strong mandate, and why they are not more magnanimous in the treatment of opponents. They would like to see rules applied to all political participants fairly, that gerrymandering be restrained. It strikes me that even as we yearn for democratic competition, competitive politics, we are asking for a kinder and gentler politics. We seem to be repulsed by the competitive, mean politics of some Western democracies.

Educated and younger Singaporeans do not want to see political overkill when the government deals with political opponents. This may be the result of the decades-long predominance of the ruling party in Parliament and in government that, as politics matures and evolves, these are the values and norms that have come to be shared by the society and community. This is who we are. Consequently, the political tools in the toolbox that worked in the past may not be acceptable or as effective going

---

[1] Pew Research Center, "The Generation Gap in American Politics," March 1, 2018, https://www.pewresearch.org/politics/2018/03/01/the-generation-gap-in-american-politics/

forward. Prime Minister Lee Hsien Loong was seen by many as gracious and honest in his reaction to the election results and his reaching out to the Workers' Party leader Pritam Singh was applauded.

Post-election, the PAP as a party would be seeking to understand the messages voters were sending in the results and, as Minister K Shanmugam said, "It requires a lot of soul-searching and reflection." I believe we will see some changes. The tone post-election was a unifying one.

This lecture is on "Singapore in a Time of Flux". Let me use the rest of my time to share with you how I see Singapore responding to the forces of change around us and challenges that are tumultuous and transformational, where political, economic, and international structures are unravelling and strategic choices to be made.

Disruption: Singapore and the COVID-19 Pandemic

Singapore was initially held up as a gold standard of how to handle the pandemic by the World Health Organisation (WHO) and the United States media — but we soon became a cautionary warning. Now that we are into the fifth month of the COVID-19 pandemic, what have we learned about Singapore and about our resilience to deal with the crisis?

In GE2020, some opposition parties made the handling of the pandemic an issue. Some mistakes were made. Singapore was not and is not the only country that is trying to get ahead of this crisis and had to change its plans as we learned more about the virus.

The pandemic has highlighted three important truths.

First, we have to come to grips with the issue of foreign workers/ migrant workers in Singapore. They are a permanent transient presence in Singapore.

For one, their large numbers and dense living will always pose risks during pandemics. Our economic growth has been dependent on raising productivity through manpower rather than productivity through use of technology. The question is to what extent and how fast we can shift the paradigm. Employers will argue, and they have a point, that the present time is not the best time to incur new costs as many companies are in grave difficulties. But sooner or later, these and more questions need to be reviewed after COVID-19 is brought under control.

In addition, the reality of the living and working conditions of foreign migrant workers in Singapore must be seriously addressed. Protocols need to be strengthened. There are moves now by the authorities to look into the housing in the dormitories to improve the space allotment for the workers. Public health would require it. Civil society organisations have been highlighting their plight consistently. Many Singaporeans now acknowledge that their situation is an embarrassment. We can and must do much better.

Second, Singaporeans have a generous heart and a strong community sense. Very many Singaporeans came forth to help lower-income families tide over this difficult period. They volunteered to ensure kids from poor families do not fall behind in their education, that they have enough to eat, and are able to cope with the mental stress of parents losing their jobs. Singaporeans also came forward to prepare meals, and collect clothes, for the foreign workers. We became a kinder nation, kinder towards one another, but most importantly our civic quotient increased overall. It demonstrates that in a crunch we will pull together.

Third, on the whole, the Singapore government has done well in its handling of the pandemic. Although there were criticisms over the explosion of cases among the foreign workers, overall, it has not drastically impacted Singapore's reputation. For a few weeks we ate humble pie, but we overcame that because the government acted decisively, took ownership of the problem and reassured the workers that their medical costs and meals would be covered by the state and that they were assured payment for their work. No other country has done as much anywhere in the world.

Importantly, we kept our death rate low and as of yesterday (July 14, 2020) there were no cases in intensive care and 161 cases in the hospital. Total active cases were 3,865.

What is less appreciated, because it happened under the radar, is the fact that we kept the supply chains open and that food imports were not disrupted during the global lockdown in the last few months and medical equipment were received.

Forbes magazine, working with a survey group that spoke to companies and non-profits, ranked one hundred safest countries in the world for COVID-19. Singapore ranked fourth, and Switzerland first. PM Lee was invited by the Austrian Chancellor, Sebastian Kurz, to an online summit on May 7 to discuss how to handle COVID-19 with Australia, the Czech Republic, Denmark, Greece, Israel and Norway. We are considered a serious participant in discussions on COVID-19.

Post-COVID-19, we must think through the lessons of this disruption for urban life and our economic life. COVID-19 has been a wake-up call for all cities to put health security as a top priority in their planning, with food security following closely. For Singapore, without a hinterland, ensuring the food and medical supply chains, and indeed all supply chains, are paramount.

COVID-19 is a bigger disruption for Singapore than most countries, with profound consequences for our economy, because Singapore is a major trading hub and a centre for communications. The United States-China trade war had started the redirecting of supply chains, but now with COVID-19 and closed borders, and the rise of self-sufficiency nationalism, we need to understand the new reconfiguration of supply chains and how that would impact Singapore. Creating jobs for Singaporeans, and helping businesses stay solvent, will be a main theme for Singapore for the next few years.

Democracy and Capitalism: Is the Singapore Governance Model Adequate for the Future?

Singapore Democracy

Singapore has been criticised for its authoritarian political system but admired for its results. Some academics write about how Singapore has disavowed liberalism or does not live up to a democratic system. Others describe it as a developmental state, the implication being that Singapore is a strong state and an interventionist one with a sole or inordinate focus on economic growth.

Before Singapore's independence, in his speeches at home and abroad Lee Kuan Yew had long voiced doubts about democracy's suitability and prospects in developing countries and new states. At independence, Singapore adopted parliamentary democracy based on the Westminster model. But right from the start, Lee Kuan Yew and his Cabinet wanted to establish a system to suit Singapore's needs.[2] They sought a model that could move quickly and facilitate the implementation of policies for the requirements of sudden statehood. The PAP opted for a unicameral legislature. They argued it would be difficult in a small country to fill two chambers with good people. The other reason simply was that to move efficiently and fast, single chambers were less cumbersome than dual chambers. The first general election in independent Singapore in 1968 produced a one-party parliament. The main opposition, the Barisan Sosialis, boycotted the election — a historical mistake for opposition politics in Singapore. The one-party parliament prevailed till 1981, when JB Jeyaretnam won the Anson by-election. During the 13 years without opposition, the PAP was accustomed to getting through the business of government speedily and efficiently in the legislature. There was every incentive to keep it that way. But they took every GE very seriously, as a referendum on their performance.

What sort of political system did we evolve and how are we faring? In an essay in 1975 entitled "Politics in an Administrative State: Where Has the Politics Gone?" I wrote of the systematic depoliticisation of Singapore politics in the 1960s and 1970s by the PAP government and the shift of politics to the bureaucracy, the technocrat-bureaucrats, where ministries and agencies debate ideas, proposals, policies and their implementation,

---

[2] Han Fook Kwang, Warren Fernandez, and Sumiko Tan, *Lee Kuan Yew: The Man and His Ideas* (Singapore: Marshall Cavendish Editions, 2015), 129–31.

without external consultation. The politicians however kept their ear to the ground through the Meet-the-People sessions and their constituency walkabouts. Inter-party politics disappeared with the rise of the dominant one-party system. Politics within the ruling party was discouraged. Civil society groups then known as interest groups were minimal. In the administrative state a strong political leadership took the lead and worked with bureaucracy to promote the development of Singapore. Later, there were changes made to have grassroots feedback consultations added but the central idea of the administrative state remained. Power was centralised and decision-making entrusted to the technocratic bureaucracy.

The repoliticisation of Singapore began in 1981 through the Anson by-election followed by the general election of 1984. In 1984 the PAP vote plunged to 62.9 per cent from 75.6 per cent in 1980. JB Jeyaretnam was re-elected to Anson and Chiam See Tong was elected to represent Potong Pasir. Gradually but surely, repoliticisation of the administrative state was taking place. The political leadership and the administrative state had to adjust to repoliticisation. After the 1984 general election, the PAP introduced the concept of the Non-Constituency Member of Parliament (NCMP), where the "best loser" candidate with the highest votes could obtain a seat in the legislature. In 1990 the Nominated Member of Parliament (NMP), a position by appointment was introduced. Both measures were meant to increase the presence of diverse voices in Parliament and diminish the need for an elected opposition.

But with the rapid changes in society, globalisation, economic success and restructuring, travel and study abroad, and the growth of a large well-educated middle class, dissatisfaction and a desire for political change mounted, then erupted. By the 2011 general election, with the convergence of several deeply felt social and economic issues, such as growing inequality and the fast-increasing numbers of foreign immigrants, Singapore's populist politics arrived. The campaign atmosphere was charged. The PAP lost its first GRC, a slate of five seats, and a SMC, both to the Workers' Party — giving the opposition party six elected seats in Parliament. The

PAP won 81 of the 87 seats and 60.1 per cent of the popular vote, its lowest vote since independence. In 2013, the Workers' Party picked up another seat in a by-election increasing its parliamentary strength to seven.

But the governing PAP had not lost its feel for policies and competition. It immediately introduced a slew of social and economic policies, strengthening safety nets, and conducted a process of consultations in 2012–2013 called *Our Singapore Conversation*. In the 2015 general election, the PAP improved its popular vote to almost 70 per cent. The importance of staying connected with a shifting political ground was the cautionary lesson of the 2011 general election. With GE2020 we see a fully repoliticised Singapore.

In the 21st century, we are now working with the Administrative State 2.0 or perhaps 3.0 post-2020. It has strengthened in many aspects, and other aspects are attenuated. The state is strong and there is a high degree of centralisation. The government's role in the economy as entrepreneur through government-linked companies (GLCs) and its subsidiaries has expanded.

Singapore has changed over the years. The Labour Force Survey in 2019 reported that 57.6 per cent of our resident labour force were diploma and degree holders. Among degree holders, 37 per cent had degrees from overseas universities and institutes of higher learning (Figure 3).[3] The number of professionals, managers, executives and technicians (PMETs) had risen to 1.3 million or 58.3 per cent of the labour force in 2019.[4]

Finding jobs and good jobs for them is an issue.

They hold certain points of view about the direction of the country and are deeply unhappy about their displacement by foreign PMETs. Their frustration is strongly expressed on social media and online platforms. A

---

[3] Manpower Research and Statistics Department. "Report: Labour Force In Singapore 2019." Ministry of Manpower Singapore, January 30, 2020, https://stats.mom.gov.sg/iMAS_PdfLibrary/mrsd_2019LabourForce_survey_findings.pdf

[4] Government of Singapore, "Oral Answer by Mrs Josephine Teo Minister for Manpower to PQ on local PMET employment outcomes," Ministry of Manpower, February 18, 2020, https://www.mom.gov.sg/newsroom/parliament-questions-and-replies/2020/0218-oral-answer-by-mrs-josephine-teo-minister-for-manpower-to-pq-on-local-pmet-employment-outcomes

Figure 3. Chart showing breakdown of resident labour force by highest qualification attained

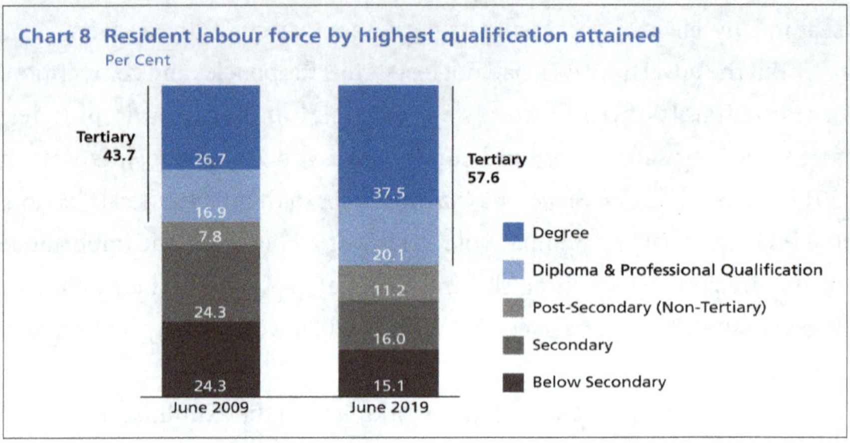

Source: Manpower Research and Statistics Department, Ministry of Manpower, "Labour Force in Singapore 2019"
Note: Data for each year may not add up to 100% due to rounding

segment seeks to contest the established consensus. Opposition parties have increased in numbers and they seem to have grown notwithstanding the limited operational room. But there is a new mushrooming of civil society organisations attracting the young, the educated and the idealistic. The civil society scene has never been more active. The recent COVID-19 pandemic shows that civil society organisations have a role to play as an early warning system for social issues and fissures in society, be it the plight of abused women, the ageing poor, or foreign workers, no matter how unwelcome the feedback. The government and these organisations can work closer together as both are interested in improving the lives of the vulnerable to build a better community.

Singapore looks to the future with the explicit ambition of harnessing the new economy and finding unconventional opportunities in a transformed post-COVID-19 world. We look for the adventurous spirit that will move us into the future economy, so we must make room for alternative views. To harvest the opportunities out there, to think the unthinkable, we must expand intellectual space giving more room for expression to encourage Singaporeans, especially young Singaporeans to be bold, to think differently, think innovatively. We should seriously discourage groupthink. In a successful bureaucracy, this is even more necessary to allow out-of-the-box thinking within. If our political model needs fixing it is how to accommodate differences and diverse views in our institutions and our country.

Singapore's democracy was challenged by its populist moment but the PAP leadership recovered from it. This does not mean that populism will not return to our politics. In the last decade the issue of inequality has been highlighted in Singapore especially as the gap seems to be widening. Discussions of rising inequality have also dominated the global political, business and academic agendas.

Will rising inequality undermine our democracy and our economic system? Let me make two points: first, about the economic system we shaped for ourselves, and second, about equality.

As the PAP leadership created a democracy that suited Singapore's needs, so they shaped the free market, capitalist model for the republic. In the beginning, the first-generation leaders were democratic socialists of the Harold Laski and British Labour Party mould, but even then Lee Kuan Yew had his ideas about the nature of human nature and the necessity of incentives. They were not orthodox socialists. They built an open and free market economy, welcomed multinational corporations, and did not buy into the welfare state, but were dedicated to providing education, jobs and housing for the people.

As the economy developed, the PAP government moved in four directions that were exceptional and came to characterise the Singapore economic model.

First, Singapore took to globalisation as a fish to water. We saw ourselves as a global city before it was fashionable to be a global city, courtesy of S Rajaratnam, our first foreign minister. We understood global supply chains. Singapore attracted multinational corporations to help us build up our skills, capabilities and networks to capital and markets.

Second, immediately after independence, the PAP government sought to eliminate confrontational industrial strikes and trade union activism associated with Singapore in the past — strong disincentives for foreign investments. They created the National Trades Union Congress (NTUC), and introduced tripartism, a platform for industry and business, union representatives and government to negotiate "orderly" wage increases.

Third, Singapore positioned the government to assume a proactive entrepreneurial role to establish enterprises, and GLCs in key sectors such as manufacturing, transport, shipbuilding, trading, services and finance, to be run as profit-making, commercial companies. This was the start of Singapore Inc., resulting in a large state presence in the economy.

Fourth, by 1974, a holding company called Temasek Holdings Private Limited was established to hold and manage assets previously held directly by the Singapore government with the purpose of allowing Temasek to own and manage these investments commercially.

Fifth, in 1981, GIC, the brainchild of Dr Goh Keng Swee, was launched. At that time the idea that a country should manage its financial reserves for its long-term future was unconventional. Nobody anywhere had ever heard of a sovereign wealth fund. Dr Goh was a brilliant mind and his knowledge of economics and finance laid a strong foundation for Singapore's economic future.

The Temasek and GIC investments benefit Singapore through the Net Investment Return Contributions (NIRC) to the annual budget. The NIRC framework allows the government to spend up to 50 per cent of long-term expected returns from our reserves. Lawrence Wong, as Second Minister of Finance, said in Parliament that these investments are now "the single largest contributor to the Government coffers."[5] These revenues can be used for social spending. Put another way, the Pioneer and Merdeka packages were paid for with the returns from Temasek and GIC investments.

---

[5] Ng Jun Sen, "Budget 2020: 'Do Not Take Our Fiscal Strength for Granted,'" says Lawrence Wong on Long-Term Pressures on NIRC," *TODAY*, February 28, 2020, https://www.todayonline.com/singapore/budget-2020-do-not-take-our-fiscal-strength-granted-says-lawrence-wong-long-term-pressures

This developmental model created the enviable economic success of Singapore, with the United Nations Development Programme (UNDP) ranking Singapore ninth in the Human Development Index 2019.[6] Critics point to flaws in the model highlighting the inequality as a troubling consequence. Inequality was an issue together with cost of living in the general election of 2011. Since then, critical social scientists have been prolific on the topic of inequality. Teo You Yenn's book, *This is What Inequality Looks Like*, was a bestseller when it was published in 2018. In fact it was interesting to see how the government ministers have come out in front of the poverty issue and in 2019 it was much discussed in Parliament and brought up in official speeches. In November, an academic from the Lee Kuan Yew School of Public Policy at the National University of Singapore did the first count of homeless people in Singapore and estimated that the numbers were between 921 to 1,050 in a study supported by the Ministry of Social and Family Development (MSF).

The PAP government's approach to equality, as then Deputy PM Tharman Shanmugaratnam explained in 2018, is to focus on social mobility — "the heart and soul of our ambition". He went on to say, "[B]efore we think of the relativities, which is what inequalities are about, we have to first think about how we can make sure that everyone moves up, including those in the broad middle of our society — the middle class."[7] There is new attention to levelling the playing field by focusing on good quality preschool education for all and cheaper and good childcare for low-income families. Successive budgets have introduced creative and thoughtful schemes to help Singaporean employers keep their workers on their jobs during times of economic crisis, upgrade their skills to be ready for Industry 4.0 and retrain themselves. There are transfers to make up for low-wage workers, subsidies targeted at the elderly poor, the disabled,

---

[6]   United Nations Development Programme, "2019 Human Development Index Ranking," 2019, http://hdr.undp.org/en/content/2019-human-development-index-ranking

[7]   Tharman Shanmugaratnam, "DPM Tharman Shanmugaratnam's Dialogue at the IPS 30th Anniversary Event," Prime Minister's Office Singapore, October 25, 2018, http://www.pmo.gov.sg/Newsroom/dpm-tharmans-dialogue-ips-30th-anniversary-event

low-income families, and in particular healthcare transfers. You know of Workfare, Silver Support, the Pioneer and Merdeka healthcare packages, the Silver Housing Bonus and the permanent GST Vouchers.

But the problem remains that there are still many individuals and families who are not aware of these schemes and do not know how to access them. Government and community workers and civil society organisations are trying to reach out to help them.

In February 2020, SingStat released the Key Household Income Trends Report for Singapore, containing very interesting data. The report shows the Gini coefficient, based on household income from work per household member was 0.452 in 2019 compared to 0.458 in 2018 and lowest since 2001. After adjusting for government transfers and taxes, the Gini coefficient fell from 0.452 to 0.398 for 2019 (Figure 4). It shows inequality has reduced, not increased.[8]

The good news is that wages of the lowest income earners are rising at a faster pace than the highest income earners. As Senior Minister Tharman Shanmugaratnam said, low-wage workers in the 20th percentile of the income ladder have seen an increase in wages of close to 40 per cent in real terms over the last 10 years (Figure 5).[9]

Figure 4. Singapore's Gini coefficient in recent years

	Before adjusting for Government transfers and taxes	After adjusting for Government transfers and taxes
2019	0.452	0.398
2018	0.458	0.404

Source: Department of Statistics Singapore, "Report on Key Household Income Trends, 2019" (https://www.singstat.gov.sg/-/media/files/publications/households/pp-s26.pdf)

---

[8] Department of Statistics, Singapore, "Press Release: Key Household Income Trends, 2019," February 20, 2020, https://www.singstat.gov.sg/-/media/files/news/press20022020.pdf

[9] Nisha Ramchandani, "Singapore's Productivity and Median Wage Have Grown by a Third in the Last 10 Years: Tharman," *The Business Times*, July 8, 2020, https://www.businesstimes.com.sg/government-economy/singapores-productivity-and-median-wage-have-grown-by-a-third-in-the-last-10

Figure 5. Statistics cited by Senior Minister Tharman Shanmugaratnam during GE2020

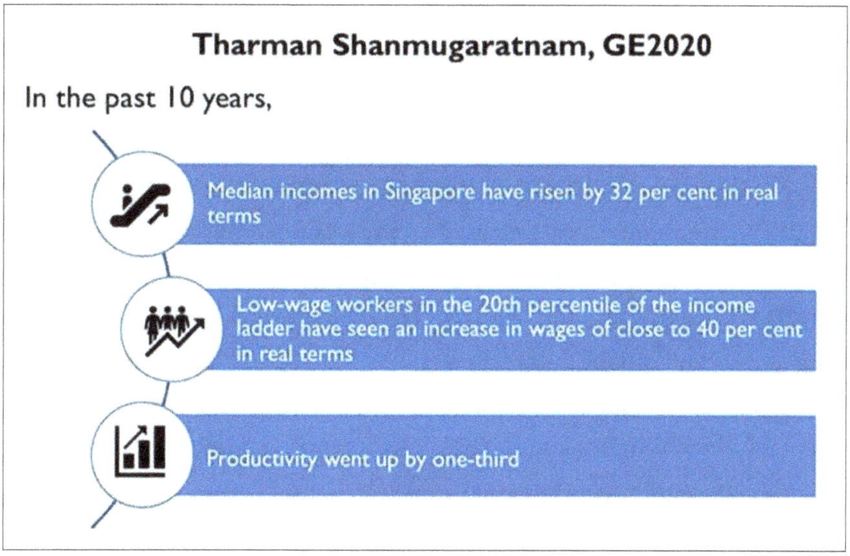

Source: Nisha Ramchandani, "Singapore's Productivity and Median Wage Have Grown by a Third in the Last 10 Years: Tharman," *The Business Times*, July 8, 2020.

Critics have frequently pointed out that Singapore has high inequality compared with other developed economies, which have lower Gini coefficients. It is true. But Singapore's figures show tentative change in the right direction compared with the industrialised democracies of the United States and Europe where incomes have stagnated or decreased.

Fortunately, in Singapore unlike other countries there is no divisive debate about providing subsidies to the needy. There are no ideological conservative parties who argue against assisting the poor; rather, the debate is on giving more, with the opposition pressing for bigger subsidies and giving to more groups. The question of raising taxes to pay the benefits is not yet part of the discourse. It will be one day.

Inequality is an issue that must be worked at constantly. In that sense Singapore is more like Europe where there is an acceptance of a social responsibility to provide for the lower income groups. The PAP does not accept the welfare state but with globalisation, disruption and the sudden collapse of the world economies, government leaders have pragmatically and sensibly accepted the need to roll out safety nets in the immediate aftermath of the Global Financial Crisis rather than to follow the West in cutting back entitlements. The response during COVID-19 suggests the understanding of societal needs. As the country becomes more affluent, basic needs for those at the bottom 20 per cent will change; they will require more just to ensure their situation does not become more dire. Now we have to worry about the squeezed middle class. The work is never done. The goalposts change all the time and so eliminating poverty is always a work in progress.

The discussion on the health of the political and economic model of Singapore would not be complete without mention of two other challenges. The first is the place and role of foreign workers in Singapore, and the second is the ability of Singapore to nurture and strengthen the presence of small and medium enterprises (SMEs).

The foreign-local conflict that is found in all societies with hyper globalisation is something that must be handled politically. The effects of COVID-19 could very well slow the movement of people for a few years, and cities and countries are redesigning themselves with "good" or "smart" density in mind. There is a limit beyond which it is not politically sustainable to maintain a huge intake of foreign population. In fact the government has been moderating the immigration, and become more selective while keeping its doors open. There is a natural attrition that will come with the pandemic recession.

The last point I wish to make about the future of the economic model of Singapore is that for our model to be sustainable more attention must be invested to strengthen and grow the small and medium-sized businesses in Singapore (SMEs), the start-ups and the gig workers. In July 2019, official statistics listed 273,100 SMEs in Singapore (Figure 6). Minister for Trade and Industry Chan Chun Sing, at the launch of the SME Academy in August 2019, shared that SMEs make up 99 per cent of all our companies, employing 72 per cent of our workforce. Together they produce 47 per cent of our GDP.[10]

---

[10] Ministry of Trade and Industry Singapore, "Speech by Minister Chan Chun Sing at the Launch of SME Leadership Academy by Google and UOB," August 5, 2019, https://www.mti.gov.sg/Newsroom/Speeches/2019/08/Speech-by-Minister-Chan-Chun-Sing-at-the-Launch-of-SME-Leadership-Academy

Figure 6. Number, employment and value-added of enterprises in 2019

Source: Department of Statistics Singapore, "Singapore Economy" infographics, 2019

One problem is that SMEs are formed but SMEs may exit too if they cannot survive. Most of them have problems with manpower, cash flow, market size and innovation. Efforts have been made by the government with many programmes and schemes to help SMEs. The 2020 budget has many assistance packages for SMEs, but they must decode the budget. The problem is communicating to the SMEs, in a language they understand, to take advantage of the help offered and the flexibility of the conditions. Implementation is important. In the civil service it is said, implementation is policy. If you have a good policy but it is not or badly implemented, you do not have a policy. So the bureaucracy has to ensure that they deliver assistance in a timely and helpful manner.

For our SMEs to do well, they must go beyond the Singapore market. Within the Singapore market it would do well for the Temasek-linked companies (TLCs) and GLCs to remember what the government said in 2004. Lim Hwee Hua, then Minister of State for Finance, told a business audience that, in line with letting private sector drive the economy, the government had a "Yellow Pages" rule. If it is in the Yellow Pages, refrain from setting up business in that area. Government should enter into strategic areas and where the private sector is not ready. That is a good rule to be revisited. Enterprise Singapore has come up with many creative packages to strengthen the SMEs, and they are working on leading business missions overseas. But I do not think it is just a matter of going overseas to see what new markets have to offer. SMEs need to strategically enter these markets. Perhaps these SMEs need the GLCs and TLCs to take a few of them on a project as consultants or contractors so that they would be able to build a track record and gain experience.

Post COVID-19, the economies globally will be in a bad shape. It is a good time to rethink. How do we help our SMEs to retool themselves for success at home and in the region?

The New Regional and Global Context

Singapore has thrived since its birth in a relatively benign and open international environment. We must now prepare ourselves for a more hostile, less generous world where nativism, nationalism and protectionism are on the rise. The trends were there but have been accelerated by the COVID-19 pandemic. Singapore is a global hub for many activities and that has been the foundation of our rapid growth. It is likely hyper globalisation will slow down. Some predict deglobalisation taking place, or a "slowbalisation". Most big countries will be tempted to turn inward. India's PM Modi told his people on May 12 that "a new era of economic self-reliance has begun", Japan's COVID-19 stimulus will give special subsidies to firms that repatriate their factories home, European Union officials speak of "strategic autonomy", and the United States urged many of its large multinational corporations to adopt onshore manufacturing.[11] We will have to read the new trends to take advantage of the new regionalisation

---

[11] "Globalisation Unwound: Has Covid-19 Killed Globalisation?" *The Economist*, May 14, 2020, https://www.economist.com/leaders/2020/05/14/has-covid-19-killed-globalisation

and regionalism. Singapore is taking a positive view that the shift in global supply chains might benefit Singapore as multinationals move their production lines to the region from China and India. Singapore should leverage its position as a financial and logistics hub with strong rule of law.

There is another source of uncertainty. The United States-China rivalry has deteriorated far faster than anyone anticipated. What will this mean for the countries in the region, for friends and allies? Can we create the space for ourselves between the giants? Before I explore the path and Singapore's position, we should examine the equities we have with each power.

From the start Singapore was a strong supporter of China's peaceful and constructive engagement with the region. There are many ongoing government-to-government projects in Suzhou, Tianjin, and Chongqing. China was our largest trade partner in 2019 with S$137.3 billion in merchandise imports and exports, while trade in services in 2018 amounted to S$35 billion. China's investments in Singapore in 2017 totalled S$36.3 billion. The Belt and Road Initiative (BRI) has been a major opportunity for co-operation in infrastructural and financial connectivity with China and opportunities for third-party collaboration. Among BRI countries, Singapore accounted for 85 per cent of total inbound investments to China, and nearly one-third of China's outbound investments to BRI countries flow through Singapore.[12] We are working with China to establish a new "Southern Transport Corridor" connecting Chongqing in West China with Beibu Gulf in Guangxi. Singapore is connecting the overland Silk Road with the Maritime Silk Road.

The United States established a presence in Singapore after they were asked to leave Subic Bay and Clark Airbase. We offered the United States access to our military facilities in a 1990 agreement, hosting Comlog Westpac in Sembawang. This agreement was renewed in September 2019 and will last till 2035. In 2005 we signed the Strategic Framework Agreement.

---

[12] Ministry of Foreign Affairs, Singapore, "MFA Press Release: Speech By Minister For Foreign Affairs Dr Vivian Balakrishnan During The Committee Of Supply Debate, 1 March 2018," March 1, 2018, http://www.mfa.gov.sg/Newsroom/Press-Statements-Transcripts-and-Photos/2018/03/Min-COS-2018-Speech

Bilateral Singapore-United States trade in merchandise goods was S$105 billion, and services amounted to S$75.3 billion.[13] United States foreign direct investment cumulative stock in Singapore in 2018 was S$296.3 billion.[14] There are 4,200 American companies in Singapore.

There is no doubt that we have substantial interests and relations with both powers, but we have never been in this place before. We have not felt the pressure and tug of war of both powers. The period of United States-China "strategic engagement" was best for the region and Singapore.

The South China Sea is increasingly where the United States and China will test their strength and influence and play out the strategic rivalry. There is no consensus among ASEAN countries on how they would respond and there is no ASEAN foreign policy or common position. It is probably true to say ASEAN countries, and all Asian countries, accept China has a right to grow into a great power, but would like to see China play by the international rules; and smaller countries would like to see China grow to be a magnanimous power.

An ISEAS-Yusof Ishak Institute Survey 2020 of ASEAN opinion makers is telling about attitudes towards the two major powers. On the question of whom they see as the most influential economic and political strategic power in Southeast Asia, China easily outpolled the United States. But the countries were also worried about this influence.

---

[13] Department of Statistics, Singapore, "Singapore International Trade," May 2020, http://www.singstat.gov.sg/modules/infographics/singapore-international-trade

[14] United States Trade Representative, "Singapore," accessed July 10, 2020, https://ustr.gov/countries-regions/southeast-asia-pacific/Singapore

Figure 7. Most influential economic powers in Southeast Asia

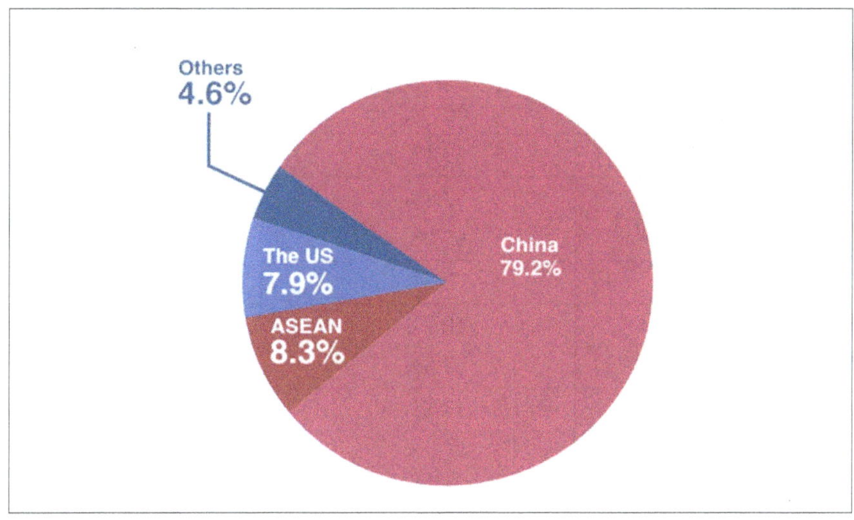

Source: ASEAN Studies Centre and ISEAS-Yusof Ishak Institute, "The State of Southeast Asia: 2020 Survey Report," p. 3.

Figure 8. Most influential political and strategic powers in Southeast Asia

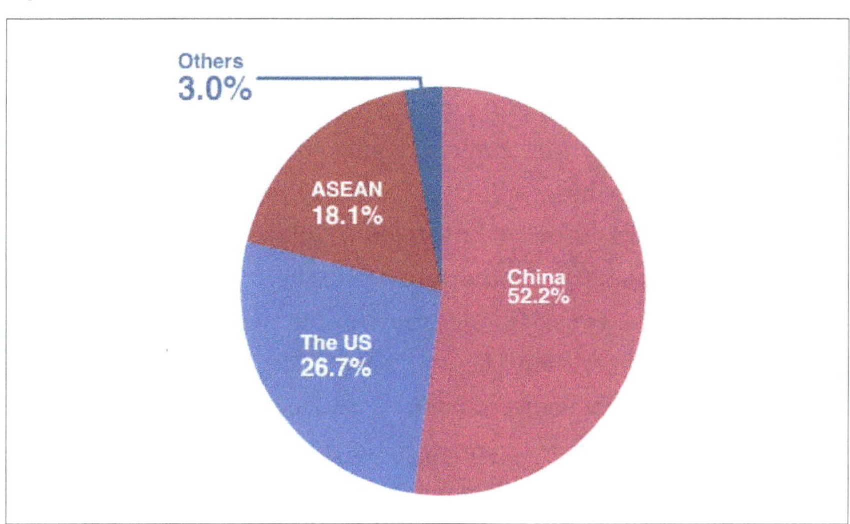

Source: ASEAN Studies Centre and ISEAS-Yusof Ishak Institute, "The State of Southeast Asia: 2020 Survey Report," p. 3.

Figure 9. If ASEAN were forced to align itself with one of the two strategic rivals, which should it choose?

Country	China	The United States
ASEAN	**46.4%**	**53.6%**
Brunei	69.1%	30.9%
Cambodia	57.7%	42.3%
Indonesia	52.0%	48.0%
Laos	73.9%	26.1%
Malaysia	60.7%	39.3%
Myanmar	61.5%	38.5%
Philippines	17.5%	82.5%
Singapore	38.7%	61.3%
Thailand	52.1%	47.9%
Vietnam	14.5%	85.5%

Source: ASEAN Studies Centre and ISEAS-Yusof Ishak Institute, "The State of Southeast Asia: 2020 Survey Report," p. 29.

An interesting fact is that though 53.6 per cent said they would choose the United States and 46.4 per cent China, the United States has just three countries — Vietnam, the Philippines and Singapore — saying they would choose to align with the United States (Figure 9). Seven of the 10 remaining ASEAN states chose China. ASEAN as a whole wanted not to make a choice but to seek out third parties to broaden their strategic space.

PM Lee in his 2019 Shangri-La Dialogue speech addressed the dilemma of choice, which is a question on the minds of the leaders of every ASEAN member state. He said, "Small states like Singapore can do little to influence the big powers, but we are not entirely without agency."[15]

He continued, "There are many opportunities for smaller countries to work together to deepen economic co-operation, strengthen regional integration and build up multilateral institutions. This way, we can

---

[15] Adrian Lim, "Shangri-La Dialogue: Small States Can Strengthen Influence by Working Together, Says Lee Hsien Loong," *The Straits Times*, June 1, 2019, https://www.straitstimes.com/politics/pm-small-states-can-strengthen-influence-by-working-together

strengthen our influence as a group, and advance a collective position on issues that matter to us, be it trade, security or technology."

What is significant is that we are seeing the emergence of a coalescence of like-minded countries who simply want to carry on doing their business, supporting their growth and development at a time when the two giants are locked in an intensifying competition with each other and narrowing the space for the medium-sized and smaller nations. They are not ideological and it is not formal; it is like-minded countries working together on specific issues.

The COVID-19 pandemic saw Singapore working with six countries, Australia, New Zealand, Canada, Chile, Myanmar and Brunei, to ensure that trade lines via land sea and air remained open for the flow of goods and essential supplies.[16] Following that, Singapore and 12 other countries pledged to maintain global links amid the pandemic. In the absence of United States global leadership, which the world could count on in the past, Canada convened a ministerial group comprising Brazil, France, Germany, Indonesia, Italy, Morocco, Mexico, Peru, Singapore, South Korea, Turkey and the United Kingdom. These countries pledged to pool their research and scientific resources and share findings. Neither the United States nor China are in the group, which is clearly taking a neutral path and to cut down the politicisation of science.

Regionalism or coalitions of a few states for very practical purposes such as how to deal with the opening up after the pandemic may point the way to newer regional subgroupings. Australia and New Zealand are discussing the formation of the Trans-Tasman bubble, including Fiji, to open up for travel, tourism and business ties. Presumably if this takes off, other countries can sign on to it, virus permitting. It is also possible that in Northeast Asia, Japan, South Korea and China could form another bubble. The economic and potential geopolitical dynamics of the overlapping membership would be interesting to watch and would have consequences.

---

[16] Ovais Subhani, "S'pore Working with 6 Nations to Ensure Supply of Essential Goods," *The Straits Times*, March 26, 2020, https://www.straitstimes.com/business/economy/spore-working-with-6-nations-to-ensure-supply-of-essential-goods

To Choose or Not to Choose?

For some time, strategic thinkers have pressed ASEAN countries to indicate which country they would choose to align with in the long run. The Trump Administration was not the first to pose this stark choice. President Bush did the same with America's war against terrorism. President Trump has now placed this question front and centre to his friends and allies, "Are you with us or against us?" The indications are that no country in Europe or Asia would like an exclusive relationship with the United States or China. The choice is not binary. All want to be able to develop relations with both powers.

As things progress, no one anticipates a grand bargain struck by either side with countries in the region at any forum. Singapore will not be put in a position to make a final choice like a marriage. Nor need it. We should not make a choice for as long as we can. Choice will be exercised by each country, to line up with the United States or China, depending on what initiatives the two powers put on the table. If the United States puts a Trans-Pacific Partnership on the table, countries will sign up for it or they will not because they cannot meet the conditions. The United States has put the Free and Open Indo Pacific (FOIP) on the table, but ASEAN is cautious. China placed the Asian Infrastructure Investment Bank (AIIB) and BRI on the table and all countries in the region signed up except for a couple, Australia and Japan.

For the next decade or two we will continue to see the United States as the preferred strategic and defence partner or friend in Asia, if it is not seen to be retrenching its interests. China will emerge as the important and sought-after economic partner but increasingly technology partner as well. Over time it will be discernible if the flavour of the region has changed perceptibly. But it will not just be about how many American or Chinese initiatives a country selects from each side. The question is whether strategic choices are more important than economic choices and are more telling. Nevertheless, increasingly it can be argued that economics and markets are hard power too and just as fundamental.

So how will Singapore do in a time of flux? I am optimistic. I believe we will walk into the future reasonably prepared. We are acutely aware of the fluid international developments and we are working with many like-minded countries. But it will be increasingly harder. If there be a Cold War 2.0 or 1.5, it will look different and alignments will be different. It will not be the old Cold War. Countries will want to have relationships with both powers.

We cannot predict the future. But we must be optimistic and active for that way we look for solutions and build a path forward. Gloom is not destiny.

Question-and-Answer Session
Moderated by Mr Bilahari Kausikan

Mr Bilahari Kausikan: Thank you Heng Chee for another masterly lecture which has given us all much food for thought. Before we take questions, Heng Chee has asked me to tell the audience that she wrote the lecture well before the recent General Election (GE) and that this is not a lecture just analysing the results of the GE. Her interests are broader, and I hope you will frame your questions with that in mind.

Before opening the virtual floor to the audience, let me exercise the moderator's privilege and ask Heng Chee the first question.

This is the third and last of your lectures. Your first lecture dealt with the fraying of global order and the pressures on the two ideological pillars of that order that were unchallenged for 25 years from 1989 when the Berlin Wall came down, to 2008 when the Global Financial Crisis broke out. Those two pillars are, of course, capitalism and democracy.

Your second lecture dealt with one symptom of the fraying of global order — the most dangerous and serious symptom — and these are the tensions that have arisen in United States-China relations, which show no sign of abating. In fact, that United States-China relations will not improve and will probably get worse over the next five to 10 years is a safe prediction, and will be so irrespective of the outcome of the November presidential elections in the United States. In your third lecture this evening, you have zeroed your focus into some aspects of what this all means for Singapore.

Now your three lectures have, as we expect of you, all been important, stimulating and insightful. But one very glaring omission struck me. Last year, you and Sharon Siddique published a very important book on Singapore's multiculturalism, *Singapore's Multiculturalism: Evolving Diversity*. But none of your lectures have mentioned, except perhaps very obliquely, the subject of your book — identity issues.

In your first lecture you quoted from the W. B. Yeats poem "The Second Coming", and it occurred to me that the rough beast that slouches invisibly but palpably through all three of your lectures is identity politics. It was both the cause and consequence of the challenge to democracy and capitalism, and the fraying of the global order. Identity is also easily recognisable in United States-China tensions and their competition has taken on rather ugly racial overtones. Of course, identity is always lurking in the background of a young city-state like Singapore, particularly when the multicultural, horizontal identity by which we have chosen to organise ourselves is so unique in our region, and increasingly assailed globally by different hierarchical conceptions of social and political organisation.

Now, I know it will take another series of lectures to do justice to the subject, but would you care to briefly rectify this omission? How will all that you have spoken about this evening and in your previous lectures affect the Singapore identity? A very simple question for you to start with.

Professor Chan Heng Chee: Thank you, Bilahari. I knew those nice things you said were just a prelude to loading this question on. You are right — I did not touch on identity because it is a very profound and large question. I chose to focus on inequality, democracy and capitalism. Of course, identity is part of the politics in the United States and Europe too. Even when you talk of foreigners versus locals it is about identity. So, identity is everywhere, as you say.

How does identity impact on Singapore? Because we are an immigrant society, there is always anxiety about the Singapore identity. The subtext is Singapore loyalty and allegiance to the country, and an individual's attitudes towards identity. I will emphasise that identity comes in layers — in each of us there are different identities. I am a Singaporean Chinese or Chinese Singaporean, and I am Singaporean in many circumstances. But I also feel Chinese in some other circumstances, like appeals to cultural programmes, culture shows — I listened to 声入人心 (*Shen Ru Ren Xin*, or *Super-Vocal*) on Chinese television, I find that quite engaging.

So one has different layers of identity and the challenge with the rise of China for Singapore is, really — where does the Chinese identity go? Where do the Chinese go with identity? And it is not just your Chinese Singaporeans. As India gets to be a great power you will find the identity of Indian Singaporeans also attracted towards India. I think Singapore Malays will be drawn to other countries too, when Indonesia becomes the full middle power that it is aspiring to be and when there is growth in Malaysia. So all communities feel tugs and pulls.

I do not think I would be alarmist about it. It is there and if the Singapore government produces good policies that win the hearts and minds of people you can in fact allow some of these pulls. People can feel drawn to other countries, but at the same time they will truly feel they are part of Singapore. I think many Singaporeans feel this.

I was interviewing a young man for the book on multiculturalism. He is a Singaporean but of Cambodian origin. He said that when he is in Cambodia he feels very Singaporean, and when he is in Singapore he feels very Cambodian. Sometimes he feels very Singaporean in Singapore and Cambodian in Cambodia. So he is a bit confused, but that is fine. I think that that is how people will be, we just have to manage it and draw the lines when lines have to be seriously drawn, but not overreact because you can put the population off.

Mr Bilahari: Thank you, Heng Chee. We have received a number of questions that have been submitted on Facebook. As predicted, they are all related to the GE but we also have some that are broader. I will summarise and try to cluster them.

The first cluster encompasses questions that get at the question, what is the greatest challenge for Singapore in uniting our people post-election? Are we generally getting more intolerant as the politics gets increasingly complicated? How do we avoid this kind of polarisation? And do you think that it is certain that a multi-party or bi-party system is going to evolve in Singapore?

Prof. Chan: Thank you, they are all very good questions that we should think about.

First of all, I still think there is a developing political culture in Singapore, which I've highlighted. Singaporeans want a kinder, gentler politics. I do not think Singaporeans want to imitate the very divisive and mean politics of the democracies of the West even when they want democracy. So that is a good start. But in competitive politics, as you get more competitive, willy-nilly, you will become more polarised. I hear younger people say, "Why should the PAP ask for a strong mandate?" But have you ever seen a political party going for elections in a democracy say, "Give me a weak mandate"?

It comes with the turf. Democracy sees some of that. But just because 10 opposition members were voted in and the opposition party had a higher vote share does not mean Singapore is divided. Please do not portray us that way. We are just maturing and there has been a healthy expression of views, and messages being sent. I do not think we are at the point of being disunited or too divisive.

How do you unify the group? Well, you cannot truly unify because those who voted for the opposition and are committed Workers' Party, PSP (Progress Singapore Party) or SDP (Singapore Democratic Party) supporters, will feel that way, and the committed PAP (People's Action Party) supporters will feel very strongly about the PAP. That is the way politics is. This is seen in many other countries, but you do not consider that divisive politics.

Does liberalism lead to intolerance? You can be too politically correct with liberalism and that is intolerant. I have seen that on some campuses in the West and I think that is not healthy. Liberalism should not lead to greater intolerance of divergent views. But people get so excited or so convinced that they are right in their liberal view that they can be illiberal towards those who do not share their view. So, yes, that is something we have to look out for. Maybe I am optimistic, but I really do not think that this is a problem we have.

Is a multi-party system good for Singapore? I think we will have a multi-party system. Frankly, the two-party system is an aberration that only the United States and Britain have. Most other democracies have many parties.

Mr Bilahari: Well, there is one geopolitical question so for a change I will ask that first before going back to the political questions. Is it possible to maintain close ties with both the United States and China going forward? I know you have addressed this in your lecture but perhaps the point you made bears repeating and emphasising.

Prof. Chan: I think this is an opportunity. How do you make choices in response to policies when the United States and China offer policies or initiatives? Do we want to sign up for them or not? How do ASEAN countries respond? On the "Free and Open Indo-Pacific", ASEAN countries are a little nervous to embrace that initiative because they see it as the containment of China. The United States is now very cleverly trying to change that a little to say it is not about China. I think in the end everyone will choose a number of policies from the United States and a number of policies from China. People will read what they want into all the initiatives. Sometimes people tell us we are too pro-United States, sometimes the Americans say we are too pro-China. So, Singapore must be right somewhere in the middle, because if we are seen by the United States as being too pro-China, and the Chinese as being too pro-United States, we are dead center.

Mr Bilahari: Absolutely. Choices in the real world are never binary. The next question is related to the point you made about avoiding or living with polarisation. How do we educate our young to live in a more complex political environment, so that the inevitable political disagreements do not get out of hand?

Prof. Chan: This was the idea in the de-ghettoisation of the HDB estates, that you do not have ethnic communities mixing only with themselves, but in truth, we do find that in schools, students often cluster if they have the same language or same ethnicity. How do you avoid group polarisation? We can only keep producing more opportunities for a class of multi-ethnicities, multi-races to be together. What is important is exposure to multiracialism and how we keep organising that. I am very glad that in recent years we have become more and more aware of multi-ethnicities, although we have to improve still on tolerance. Not everyone has the same tolerance or think of different ethnicities other than their own in the same positive way, and that we have got to try to change.

The problem is, in this digital world, we are all just going into the websites and the chat groups of maybe our own kind, our own values, our own politics. So we are quite siloed. How do you break through those silos, which are building up with technology and the digital world? I think it is a very serious question.

It is a whole bunch of actions, not just one action. It has to happen in school, it has to happen in the social space. And I am always very aware of ensuring that we have diversity when we hire, when we have a party, when we have speakers on a platform. But I cannot say everyone shares the same kind of reflex.

I remember walking into an event on an American campus organised by Singapore for Singaporeans. I walked in, looked around, and said, "Why are there so few minorities here?" The organiser did not think of it. They just allowed everybody to register and did not go out of the way to make sure that there was a broad representation. So the point is, be aware of the issue, work for it, increase the social spaces for engagement, and you hope that in time we learn. I like to think of younger people as more liberal, more multi-ethnic, inter-ethnic, but there is also a number of younger people that live in their own separate siloed worlds.

Mr Bilahari: Are Singaporeans being too critical of good governance or insufficiently appreciative of good governance? Another related question is, did the "flight to safety" mechanism fail because of the PAP's real or perceived failings in handling COVID-19, or does this represent a broader shift in attitudes regarding what we want and can accept in a government or in a crisis? In other words, is good governance underrated now or not enough?

Prof. Chan: A short and easy answer is that we have taken good governance for granted because we have had good governance all the time. One way to know it is when you travel out of Singapore, or live in a different society, I am constantly being told in the United States what a wonderful government we have and they say, "We wish we could have your government".

In Singapore, Singaporeans are very critical of government. People point to all the little pockmarks on the face. I think we just got used to good governance and we take good governance for granted. Of course, the best lesson is when you start having bad governance. But I hope we never get to that point.

The values that are being emphasised even by some of the opposition parties show that they understand what good governance entails. The fact that the Workers' Party is very much a moderate party and like the PAP — I know they do not want to be known as that, but they do not want to differ too much — means they understand what are the values at stake and what a large proportion of Singaporeans value, and that must include all the principles that make up good governance.

But we should not see an election like this as a rejection of good governance either. It is an election where grievances were there, people were losing jobs and their businesses were in trouble. Also, many people believed the PAP would win anyway. Many of us received all those bookie announcements — I saw a couple which said the PAP would sweep everything, and there were other bookie announcements where they said that the opposition will sweep everything. So there is a lot of disinformation being circulated pre-election.

But I think Singaporeans knew they would have the PAP in government, so you are assured of safety and incumbency. But they do yearn to have an opposition voice in Parliament. I think the results show that, and younger Singaporeans show that they value this. Now, frankly, if the PAP were ever in a position where the seats in Parliament become — you have 83 (PAP) seats now, let us say it gets to about 30 opposition seats in Parliament — people will think very carefully when they vote.

If the opposition parties come up to expectations, well, people will say, "Let's see". But if their performance is not good, there will be more appreciation for what the PAP offered as good governance again. But then the PAP could also get complacent and not attend to what they have attended to in the past. In that case, they would be in a tight spot.

Mr Bilahari: Now, a cluster of questions that deals with politics and public institutions. First, as a member of the Constitutional Commission to review the Elected Presidency, do you think you would review it the same way again? Next, do you think we should do away with the GRCs (Group Representative Constituencies) and revert to a system of all SMCs (Single Member Constituencies)? Finally, you have talked about the administrative state. How do you think, or do you think the civil service needs to evolve to deal with this new political situation?

Prof. Chan: If you read the report of the Constitutional Commission, you will find that there is a provision where we said, of course we can move away from the Elected Presidency and go towards Parliament appointing as we did in the past — that was one way you can ensure that ethnic groups will all be given fair representation. I want to add that it has always been my view that the presidency of Singapore should in fact rotate and that different ethnic groups must have an opportunity to occupy that seat because the presidency of the country is a unifying symbol of the country and it must represent what the country looks like in terms of its demography and ethnicity. Would I have done the same? It is never a good policy to answer questions about whether I would have done the same thing in the past. So, I do not want to answer that. But I would say, if you look at the Constitutional Commission report, it did add the proviso that there is another way of doing it, although the report did recommend the reserved election for the Elected Presidency.

Moving on to the second question about GRCs and SMCs, one should never change constitutions and constitutional provisions too often. As for political electoral arrangements, gerrymandering is what every country does but you cannot do it too blatantly. I think that has to be changed. But to change the GRC system now and make it all SMCs, you are chopping and changing too fast. I think there is some merit to GRCs because it was introduced to ensure that there is minority representation. Also, it does not only help the governing party. It helped the opposition win five seats in Aljunied, four seats in Sengkang. Otherwise you have got to go slowly, one at a time — a much harder exercise.

I do not feel strongly about whether we keep GRCs or not. I thought the reason that we had GRCs — so that we can ensure minority representation — was a good one for me when it was introduced and I do not see the reason to take it away.

On the civil service and the administrative state, I think that the civil service in Singapore, when they implement and when they make policies, needs to really think very hard and make sure we do not allow groupthink to infect us. We have got to do that self-check ourselves and when we are implementing policies we should do it with a human heart and a human touch. It is not just going by the playbook because this is the standard operating procedure (SOP) and because we are so worried about exercising discretion or being challenged. When we implement policies, we should do it intelligently with a feel for the ground.

Mr Bilahari: I will go to a cluster of questions on economic development. What are some of the undesirable developments you have observed, which might render Singapore irrelevant or less relevant in the global economy? Related to that, what principles should we adopt in restructuring our economy, to further improve on the version of democracy that we have in Singapore? A very specific question for you, wearing your cities hat — will the Jurong Central Business District (CBD) continue to be worked on, given the challenges of the recession we are in now?

Prof. Chan: Now let me take the first question first — what are some of the undesirable forces that are emerging, which will impact on Singapore's position? As a global city in the global economy, and with COVID-19 in the picture, as I said in my lecture, countries are becoming more protectionist, they practise nationalism and they want to bring many industries back home, pursue self-sufficiency. The thinking behind this is that supply chains can be broken, so you might as well start producing everything yourself at home. It really is not a good economic argument because then you do not become competitive and you are paying very high prices.

But that is happening a bit and we will have to see how far redirection and reconfiguration of supply chains go. That is what we have to watch very carefully to see how to capitalise or make sure Singapore benefits from it economically. We need to have a sense of what is happening in the region, in international politics, and we need to have relationships and networks. When I say that Singapore's reputation has not been affected that much, I mean that Singapore has done well because the Singapore brand is strong, and we are seen to be competent. We have solutions, we are able to do quality work and we are able to deliver efficiently, and that is not just the political leaders who have the plans and policies, but more generally, Singaporeans working together to produce these results.

So long as we are seen in this positive light, we will still be able to persuade others that it is not such a bad thing to locate your headquarters and turn your supply chain, make a stop in Singapore. We can still make those arguments. So we have to burnish our brand, and not just be brand proud for the sake of being brand proud.

I am brand proud and conscious for a purpose. It is for the people, you do business, you go to universities and you make your living in the world because of the Singapore brand. And that is why we must all work to preserve that brand. So in this instance of the redirection of the supply chains and what we can do in a much more competitive and, in a way, selfish world, we have to keep showing that Singapore can deliver the results, we are efficient, we are honest, and we can still keep a part of the business.

As for the Jurong CBD, frankly, I am not in a position to answer that question. But I will say this. The interesting thing about the PAP government and the PAP leadership is that in a way we never let a crisis go to waste. There is a crisis, an economic downturn, we invest, we build, we do that first while the prices are low, so you are ready when businesses come and the recovery takes place. So I would think that maybe they will keep up with the business district because it is stimulating the economy, creating jobs. As for what they build, how to design the business district, I am not in conversations about this, but I think this is how government will think, because this is how they thought in the past — they may rejig the business district in a certain way. There are a lot of people in the cities space who are asking, do you need so much office space? That is another group of questions on the redesign of the business district, but I am sure government planners will be thinking these questions, and I do not see them stopping simply because there is a big downturn.

Mr Bilahari: We have here a cluster of questions on globalisation. I am going to try to summarise them. With globalisation, do you think the nation-state will endure? Related to that, there seems to be a lack of global leadership right now. When any major political power takes an initiative, it is opposed by some other major power or it appears that way. And, historically, Singapore's geographic location was a crucial factor. Is that still going to be a crucial factor, going forward?

Prof. Chan: I will take the last question first. Is it location that has helped us? Singapore is a global city. Will we be bypassed? People who read and analyse global cities will point out that if a global city such as Singapore develops a number of activities and agglomerates activities and develops specialisation, then it becomes so inevitable that you are the go-to place, you keep your position and people, companies will make a stop because you are the place to be.

If you think of it that way, Singapore has agglomerated its activities very well, no matter whether it is shipping, communications, oil, banking, you have a whole slew of ancillary activities around an industry that builds up the importance of that industry. Now that will make it hard to shake things off.

Will our location ever be irrelevant? Will we be made irrelevant? That is a question that is always asked, and I have told many people overseas that the Singapore Cabinet must be the only Cabinet in the world that read John Norwich's *A History of Venice*, this big thick book, in the 1980s. Because what happened to Venice could happen to us and we can be made irrelevant.

So we must always find out what is the important trend, what is the important technological development so that you are not blindsided. I think that is what Singapore has to do and that is what the PAP government has been doing — how not to be blindsided, to anticipate what is happening.

But you never know. Honolulu was bypassed when long-haul carriers were introduced and airlines did not have to stop in Honolulu anymore for transpacific flights going to the United States. So, in Singapore, we must always find out what technology can render us obsolete, and also what will come up instead, the new wave of economic activities and different kinds of technology.

So maybe in the future, it will not be location, location and location, but we could have location as the digital hub, and that is a different kind of location.

On global leadership, yes, there is a lack of global leadership and I think it is very difficult to govern well today because the world has gotten so complex. We always look back to World War II which produced all your giants — or we thought they were giants. Now some people want to pull down Winston Churchill's statue, but Churchill is considered a giant. Roosevelt. Even Stalin is a giant in the Soviet Union, but, of course, there are so many negatives there. But there were giants at a particular time in history. Today, the world is getting very complex, so it is very hard to see giants stride across the stage. It is not easy to be a powerful global leader with things getting so complex. We really have to come to grips with technology and how disruptive technology can be, and how technology can reshape society, so that it is hard for those in government to try to connect with society. That is why I said that the disruption caused by technology is greater than the disruption caused by COVID-19 in my first lecture. So yes, there is a lack of global leadership but through regional groupings, countries are trying to come together to make up for that deficit by offering regional leadership

With globalisation, will the nation-state endure? We first thought that with globalisation, we will be one global community. We found that was not true. With globalisation, there was greater turning inwards and an emphasis on localisation. When you are so global, you lose your identity, and you do not know where you belong. So, people yearn for their own distinctive identity in the country or in the tribe. That is the other face of globalisation — localisation.

Will the nation-states endure and survive? I am a political scientist. I believe in multilateralism, but I also think nation-states will survive. Look at the projects of multilateralism. Europe — you find that the nation-state is alive and well, but they also share certain common European projects. The nation-state is in fact very strong, and with this new politics we talk of a resurgence of nationalism. It is not just in Asia that you see nationalism. "America First" is a new nationalism, every country has a country first policy. So nationalism is alive and well.

Mr Bilahari: I will take one last question, which is a very broad one. The question is, what hopes can we have, and what future aspirations should we encourage, for our grandchildren here in Singapore? That is probably a good note on which to end.

Prof. Chan: I would like to say good things, but I am thinking of some of the climate change hazards that will arrive. Combined with other tensions, we will face a very difficult world. So what can we hope for for our grandchildren? That they will have tolerance, and learn to work and cooperate with one another. I think by doing so, they can enhance the chances of surviving in a very difficult world.

Bibliography

Allison, Graham. "Thucydides Trap: Are the U.S. and China Headed for War?" *The Atlantic*, 24 September 2015. https://www.theatlantic.com/international/archive/2015/09/united-states-china-war-thucydides-trap/406756/

Allison, Graham T., Robert D. Blackwill, and Ali Wyne. "The Future of China." In *Lee Kuan Yew: The Grand Master's Insights on China, the United States, and the World*, edited by Ali Wyne, Graham T. Allison, and Robert Blackwill, 1–18. Cambridge, Massachusetts: MIT Press, 2013.

ASEAN Studies Centre and ISEAS-Yusof Ishak Institute. "The State of Southeast Asia: 2020 Survey Report." January 16, 2020. https://www.iseas.edu.sg/wp-content/uploads/pdfs/TheStateofSEASurveyReport_2020.pdf

Bader, Jeffrey A. "U.S.-China Relations: Is It Time to End the Engagement?" *Policy Brief Series on The New Geopolitics*, Brookings Institution, September 2018. https://www.brookings.edu/research/u-s-china-relations-is-it-time-to-end-the-engagement/

Batty, Michael, Jesse Bricker, Joseph Briggs, Elizabeth Holmquist, Susan McIntosh, Kevin Moore, Eric Nielsen, Sarah Reber, Molly Shatto, Kamila Sommer, Tom Sweeney, and Alice Henriques Volz. "Introducing the Distributional Financial Accounts of the United States," *Finance and Economics Discussion Series 2019-017*. Washington: Board of Governors of the Federal Reserve System, 2019. https://doi.org/10.17016/FEDS.2019.017

BBC World Service. "Yuval Noah Harari: Covid-19 — a new regime of surveillance?" *HARDtalk*, 23:00. April 27, 2020. https://www.bbc.co.uk/sounds/play/w3cszc1p

Bush, Richard C. "Taiwan's President Begins Her Second Term with a Call for Unity." *Brookings Institution: Order from Chaos* (blog), May 21, 2020. https://www.brookings.edu/blog/order-from-chaos/2020/05/21/taiwans-president-begins-her-second-term-with-a-call-for-unity/

Castells, Manuel. *Rupture: The Crisis of Liberal Democracy.* Translated by Rosie Marteau. Cambridge, UK: Polity Press, 2018.

Channel 4 News. "'People Very Quickly Adapted to a Very Radical Disruption' — Writer Malcolm Gladwell on Coronavirus." YouTube Video, 11:33. April 28, 2020. https://www.youtube.com/watch?v=BgydC490NG4

Clifford, Catherine. "Hedge Fund Billionaire Ray Dalio: 'Capitalism Basically Is Not Working for the Majority of People.'" CNBC, January 16, 2019. https://www.cnbc.com/2019/01/16/bridgewaters-ray-dalio-capitalism-is-not-working-for-most-people.html

Delclós, Carlos. "Spain Has a Democratic Problem — the People Have Outgrown Its Political System." *The Guardian*, September 26, 2019.

Department of Statistics, Singapore. "Press Release: Key Household Income Trends, 2019." February 20, 2020. https://www.singstat.gov.sg/-/media/files/news/press20022020.pdf

Department of Statistics, Singapore. "Singapore Economy." [2019 data]. Accessed July 10, 2020. https://www.singstat.gov.sg/modules/infographics/economy

Department of Statistics, Singapore. "Singapore International Trade." May 2020. http://www.singstat.gov.sg/modules/infographics/singapore-international-trade

Edelman. *Edelman Trust Barometer 2020*. January 19, 2020. https://www.edelman.com/sites/g/files/aatuss191/files/2020-01/2020%20Edelman%20Trust%20Barometer%20Global%20Report_LIVE.pdf

Feldstein, Steven. "The Global Expansion of AI Surveillance." Working Paper, Carnegie Endowment for International Peace, September 17, 2019. https://carnegieendowment.org/files/WP-Feldstein-AISurveillance_final1.pdf

Fukuyama, Francis. "The End of History?" *The National Interest*, no. 16 (1989): 3–18.

Fukuyama, Francis. *Trust: The Social Virtues and the Creation of Prosperity.* New York: The Free Press, 1995.

"Full text of Xi Jinping's report at 19th CPC National Congress." *Xinhua,* November 4, 2017. https://www.chinadaily.com.cn/china/19thcpcnationalcongress/2017-11/04/content_34115212.htm

Gilsinan, Kathy. "How the U.S. Could Lose a War With China." *The Atlantic,* July 25, 2019.

Grayling, A. C. *Democracy and Its Crisis.* London: Oneworld Publications, 2017.

"Globalisation Unwound: Has Covid-19 Killed Globalisation?" *The Economist,* May 14, 2020. https://www.economist.com/leaders/2020/05/14/has-covid-19-killed-globalisation

Government of Singapore. "Oral Answer by Mrs Josephine Teo Minister for Manpower to PQ on local PMET employment outcomes." Ministry of Manpower, February 18, 2020. https://www.mom.gov.sg/newsroom/parliament-questions-and-replies/2020/0218-oral-answer-by-mrs-josephine-teo-minister-for-manpower-to-pq-on-local-pmet-employment-outcomes

Han, Fook Kwang, Warren Fernandez, and Sumiko Tan. *Lee Kuan Yew: The Man and His Ideas.* Singapore: Marshall Cavendish Editions, 2015.

Hubbard, Glenn. "America Needs to Fix Capitalism to Save It." Open Future Initiative, *The Economist,* October 18, 2019. https://www.economist.com/open-future/2019/10/18/america-needs-to-fix-capitalism-to-save-it

Institute of International Strategic Studies. *The Military Balance 2020.* New York: Routledge, 2020.

Kent, David. "The Countries Where People are Most Dissatisfied with How Democracy is Working." Pew Research Center, May 31, 2019. https://www.pewresearch.org/fact-tank/2019/05/31/the-countries-where-people-are-most-dissatisfied-with-how-democracy-is-working/

Kissinger, Henry. *On China*. New York: Penguin Press, 2011.

Kissinger, Henry. *Does America Need a Foreign Policy? Toward a Diplomacy for the 21st Century*. New York: Simon & Schuster, 2002.

Knowlton, Brian. "Bush Warns Taiwan to Keep Status Quo: China Welcomes U.S. Stance." *The New York Times*, December 10, 2003. https://www.nytimes.com/2003/12/10/news/bush-warns-taiwan-to-keep-status-quo-china-welcomes-us-stance.html

Kuttner, Robert. *Can Democracy Survive Global Capitalism?* New York: W. W. Norton & Company, 2018.

Levitsky, Steven, and Daniel Ziblatt. *How Democracies Die*. New York: Crown, 2018.

Lim, Adrian. "Shangri-La Dialogue: Small States Can Strengthen Influence by Working Together, Says Lee Hsien Loong." *The Straits Times*, June 1, 2019. https://www.straitstimes.com/politics/pm-small-states-can-strengthen-influence-by-working-together

Lowy Institute. *Lowy Institute Asia Power Index 2019*. May 29, 2019.

Manpower Research and Statistics Department. "Report: Labour Force In Singapore 2019." Ministry of Manpower Singapore, January 30, 2020. https://stats.mom.gov.sg/iMAS_PdfLibrary/mrsd_2019LabourForce_survey_findings.pdf

MacLean, Nancy. *Democracy in Chains: The Deep History of the Radical Right's Stealth Plan for America*. New York: Scribe Publications, 2017.

McGregor, Richard. *Asia's Reckoning: China, Japan, and the Fate of U.S. Power in the Pacific Century*. New York: Viking, 2017.

Mearsheimer, John J. "Bound to Fail: The Rise and Fall of the Liberal International Order." *International Security* 43, no. 4 (Spring 2019): 7–50. https://doi.org/10.1162/isec_a_00342

Milanovic, Branko. "The Clash of Capitalisms: The Real Fight for the Global Economy's Future." *Foreign Affairs*, January/February 2020.

Ministry of Foreign Affairs, Singapore. "MFA Press Release: Speech By Minister For Foreign Affairs Dr Vivian Balakrishnan During The Committee Of Supply Debate, 1 March 2018." March 1, 2018. http://www.mfa.gov.sg/Newsroom/Press-Statements-Transcripts-and-Photos/2018/03/Min-COS-2018-Speech

Ministry of Trade and Industry Singapore. "Speech by Minister Chan Chun Sing at the Launch of SME Leadership Academy by Google and UOB." August 5, 2019. https://www.mti.gov.sg/Newsroom/Speeches/2019/08/Speech-by-Minister-Chan-Chun-Sing-at-the-Launch-of-SME-Leadership-Academy

Newport, Frank. "Democrats More Positive About Socialism Than Capitalism." Gallup, August 31, 2018. https://news.gallup.com/poll/240725/democrats-positive-socialism-capitalism.aspx

Ng, Jun Sen. "Budget 2020: 'Do Not Take Our Fiscal Strength for Granted,'" says Lawrence Wong on Long-Term Pressures on NIRC." *TODAY*, February 28, 2020. https://www.todayonline.com/singapore/budget-2020-do-not-take-our-fiscal-strength-granted-says-lawrence-wong-long-term-pressures

Nixon, Richard M. "Asia after Viet Nam." *Foreign Affairs*, October 1967. https://www.foreignaffairs.com/articles/asia/1967-10-01/asia-after-viet-nam.

Office for National Statistics. "Total Wealth in Great Britain: April 2016 to March 2018." Total Wealth in Great Britain — Office for National Statistics, December 5, 2019. https://www.ons.gov.uk/peoplepopulationandcommunity/personalandhouseholdfinances/incomeandwealth/bulletins/totalwealthingreatbritain/april2016tomarch2018

Runciman, David. *How Democracy Ends.* London: Profile Books, 2018.

Shambaugh, David. *China's Future.* Cambridge, UK; Malden, MA: Polity Press, 2016.

Strategy Group (Prime Minister's Office Singapore), Department of Statistics, Ministry of Home Affairs, Immigration & Checkpoints Authority, Ministry of Manpower. *Population in Brief 2019.* September 2019. https://www.strategygroup.gov.sg/files/media-centre/publications/population-in-brief-2019.pdf

Shanmugaratnam, Tharman. "DPM Tharman Shanmugaratnam's Dialogue at the IPS 30th Anniversary Event." Prime Minister's Office Singapore, October 25, 2018. http://www.pmo.gov.sg/Newsroom/dpm-tharmans-dialogue-ips-30th-anniversary-event

Shepardson, David, Karen Freifeld, and Alexandra Alper. "U.S. Moves to Cut Huawei off from Global Chip Suppliers as China Eyes Retaliation." *Reuters*, May 15, 2020. https://in.reuters.com/article/us-usa-huawei-tech-exclusive/u-s-moves-to-cut-huawei-off-from-global-chip-suppliers-as-china-eyes-retaliation-idINKBN22R1KC

Subhani, Ovais. "S'pore Working with 6 Nations to Ensure Supply of Essential Goods." *The Straits Times*, March 26, 2020. https://www.straitstimes.com/business/economy/spore-working-with-6-nations-to-ensure-supply-of-essential-goods

Swanson, Ana, and David McCabe. "Trump Effort to Keep U.S. Tech Out of China Alarms American Firms." *The New York Times*, February 16, 2020. https://www.nytimes.com/2020/02/16/business/economy/us-china-technology.html

Tang, Shiping. "China and the Future International Order(s)." *Ethics & International Affairs* 32, no. 1 (2018): 31–43. https://doi.org/10.1017/S0892679418000008

Tham, Yuen-C. "China Does Not Want to Vie for No. 1 Position: Chinese Defence Minister Wei Fenghe." *The Straits Times*, June 2, 2019. https://www.straitstimes.com/singapore/china-does-not-want-to-vie-for-number-1-position-chinese-defence-minister-wei-fenghe

Triolo, Paul. "US-China Competition: The Coming Decoupling?" *RSIS Commentary*, October 23, 2019. https://www.rsis.edu.sg/rsis-publication/rsis/geopolitics-and-technology-us-china-competition-the-coming-decoupling/#.X4W3-9AzY2w

"Trump Accuses China of 'Raping' US with Unfair Trade Policy." BBC News, May 2, 2016. https://www.bbc.com/news/election-us-2016-36185012

United Nations Development Programme. "2019 Human Development Index Ranking." 2019. http://hdr.undp.org/en/content/2019-human-development-index-ranking

United States National Security & Defense. "National Security Strategy of the United States of America." White House, December 18, 2017, https://www.whitehouse.gov/wp-content/uploads/2017/12/NSS-Final-12-18-2017-0905-2.pdf

United States National Security Council. "United States Strategic Approach to the People's Republic of China." White House, May 26, 2020. https://www.whitehouse.gov/wp-content/uploads/2020/05/U.S.-Strategic-Approach-to-The-Peoples-Republic-of-China-Report-5.20.20.pdf

United States Trade Representative. "Singapore." Accessed July 10, 2020. https://ustr.gov/countries-regions/southeast-asia-pacific/Singapore

U.S. Congress, United States-China Economic and Security Review Commission. *Hearing on a "World-Class" Military: Assessing China's Global Military Ambitions before the U.S.-China Economic and Security Review Commission.* 116th Congress, 1st session, June 20, 2019.

White, Hugh. *The China Choice: Why America Should Share Power*. Melbourne: Black Inc., 2013.

Wike, Richard, and Shannon Schumacher. "Democratic Rights Popular Globally but Commitment to Them Not Always Strong." *Spring 2019 Global Attitudes Survey*. Pew Research Center, February 27, 2020. https://www.pewresearch.org/global/2020/02/27/attitudes-toward-elected-officials-voting-and-the-state/

Yeo, George. "24th Gordon Arthur Ransome Oration: Human Solidarity in a Fragmenting World." January 18, 2020. https://www.ams.edu.sg/view-pdf.aspx?file=media%5C5215_fi_887.pdf&ofile=24th+GAR+Oration_George+Yeo.pdf

Zakaria, Fareed. *The Future of Freedom*. New York: W. W. Norton & Company, 2007.

Zhao, Minghao. "Is a New Cold War Inevitable? Chinese Perspectives on US-China Strategic Competition." *Chinese Journal of International Politics* 12, no. 3(2019): 377, https://doi.org/10.1093/cjip/poz010

Zoellick, Robert. "Whither China: From Membership to Responsibility?" U.S. Department of State Archive, September 21, 2005. https://2001-2009.state.gov/s/d/former/zoellick/rem/53682.htm

Index

CPSIA information can be obtained
at www.ICGtesting.com
Printed in the USA
JSHW021626020221
11459JS00001B/37

Padilla, Christopher. "IBM Urges Commerce Department to Adjust Approach on IT Supply Chain Security." IBM THINKPolicy Blog, 10 January 2020. https://www.ibm.com/blogs/policy/supply-chain-rule/

Paulson, Jr., Henry M. "Remarks by Henry M. Paulson, Jr., on the United States and China at a Crossroads, at the Bloomberg New Economy Forum in Singapore." Paulson Institute, November 7, 2018. https://www.paulsoninstitute.org/press_release/remarks-by-henry-m-paulson-jr-on-the-united-states-and-china-at-a-crossroads/

Pew Research Center. "The Generation Gap in American Politics." March 1, 2018. https://www.pewresearch.org/politics/2018/03/01/the-generation-gap-in-american-politics/

Piketty, Thomas. *Capital in the Twenty-First Century*. Translated by Arthur Goldhammer. Cambridge, Massachusetts: Belknap Press of Harvard University Press, 2014.

"Premier Li Keqiang Meets the Press: Full Transcript of Questions and Answers." *China Daily*, May 30, 2020. https://www.chinadaily.com.cn/a/202005/30/WS5ed1b75fa310a8b241159989.html

Ramchandani, Nisha. "Singapore's Productivity and Median Wage Have Grown by a Third in the Last 10 Years: Tharman." *The Business Times*, July 8, 2020. https://www.businesstimes.com.sg/government-economy/singapores-productivity-and-median-wage-have-grown-by-a-third-in-the-last-10

Reinhart, Carmen M., and Kenneth S. Rogoff. *This Time Is Different: Eight Centuries of Financial Folly*. Princeton, NJ: Princeton University Press, 2009.

Rudd, Kevin. "The Avoidable War: Reflections on U.S.-China Relations and the End of Strategic Engagement," Asia Society Policy Institute, January 21, 2019.